Andrew J. Rickoff

Past and Present of Our Common School Education

Reply to President B. A. Hinsdale, with a brief sketch of the history of

elementary education in America

Andrew J. Rickoff

Past and Present of Our Common School Education
Reply to President B. A. Hinsdale, with a brief sketch of the history of elementary education in America

ISBN/EAN: 9783337096731

Printed in Europe, USA, Canada, Australia, Japan

Cover: Foto ©Andreas Hilbeck / pixelio.de

More available books at **www.hansebooks.com**

PAST AND PRESENT

OF

Our Common School Education.

REPLY TO PRESIDENT B. A. HINSDALE,

WITH

A Brief Sketch of the History

OF

ELEMENTARY EDUCATION IN AMERICA.

BY ANDR. J. RICKOFF,

SUPERINTENDENT OF SCHOOLS, CLEVELAND.

PUBLISHED BY ORDER OF THE NORTH-EASTERN OHIO
TEACHERS' ASSOCIATION

CLEVELAND, O:
LEADER PRINTING COMPANY, 146 SUPERIOR STREET.
1877.

INTRODUCTION.

It having been understood that President HINSDALE had some severe strictures to make concerning the graded common schools of the day, he was invited to read a paper on the subject at the meeting of this Association which was held December 9th, 1876. The address was listened to with great interest; and though there were few, if any, who adopted his views, a copy of the paper was solicited for publication. It was generally felt that the President had made the strongest possible presentation of the floating criticisms of the day; and the way in which it has been received by the public, proves that it is acceptable to those who hold views in anywise like his own. Certain it is, that his commentators have added little or nothing to his arguments or *repértoire* of facts to sustain the position which he has taken.

The delay of this reply has been attributed by some to that timidity which is naturally felt in attacking a strong antagonist; but it is believed that this paper will show that the natural advantage of our position is so great that it really requires no moral courage or forensic skill to defend it against any arguments that have been or may be brought against it. The truth is, that I hesitated greatly to accept the duty imposed on me by the Executive Committee, because it seemed impossible for me to get the time necessary to make myself certain as to the facts involved in the discussion, and to prepare such a paper as might be acceptable to my highly respected associates. The result has proved that my apprehensions were correct. I have been unable to prepare my reply for the press till now—more than six months since its delivery.

Just here, and once for all, let me say that I shall aim to speak as an advocate for the best education of the people, and not as a partisan of the schools. I do not claim that the graded schools are perfect, or that they are as good as they can be made. It would be wonderful if mistakes were not made here as elsewhere in the affairs of men. I only claim that they are better than they have been at any previous period of their history, and what is still more encouraging, that they are rapidly improving. I might justly claim also that the improvement of the common schools and the establishment of the High and Normal Schools have been mighty incentives and aids to the improvement of private schools, academies and even colleges, but it is not necessary to raise that question here.

I do not wish to be understood to deny that there have been good schools in the past, for wherever there have been good school-masters there have been good schools. From the first there have been men in New England and in every State of the Union who have been good educators. They taught

well whatever they attempted to teach; but the evidence which I shall submit
will show that they arose above the common level by the force of superior
manhood, and not by the aid of their surroundings.   It would seem hardly
necessary to caution the reader against too wide a deduction from his own
limited experience.   Because one's neighbor is an intemperate man, it is
hardly safe to say that intemperance is the habit of the community; so, if
one's schoolmaster chanced to be a good one, it is not certain that in the time
of his youth the education of the whole State was in good hands, or even that
good teachers were common.

One more paragraph and we are done with prefatory remarks.   It does not
seem best to confine myself to a mere answer to Mr. HINSDALE.   The evidence of a few competent witnesses and a thorough refutation of his West
Point argument would be sufficient to meet every material point in his address.
But I shall avail myself of the opportunity to direct public attention to such
facts in the history of the common schools as may be of service in their
present and future management.   The question, of overcrowding the course of ·
study being raised, it will be quite appropriate to show that that overcrowding
comes from the undue expansion of those branches which are honored with
the name of common school studies, not from the introduction of what are
styled the higher branches of education.   General SHERMAN'S and Professor
CHURCH'S views on this subject, as quoted by President HINSDALE, are
superficial in the extreme.

OUR COMMON SCHOOL EDUCATION.

———

THAT the reader may be able to keep in mind the course of Mr. HINSDALE'S argument, I shall, as I go along, present outlines of his discourse, under what seem to me appropriate heads. I hope that they may be accepted as fair — I certainly design that they shall be. I shall aim to preserve as much as possible the force and spirit of the original, to which the reader is referred, if any point seems to be unfairly stated.

1. "In no country has the common school taken deeper root than in our own." "Though we may not be equal to others in our liberal, technical and art culture, we yield to none in our devotion to popular elementary instruction."

2. "Its influence"—that is, of the common school system—"in the promotion of intelligence and prosperity in the Northern and Eastern States has been rated so high, that every new State adopts it without question."—(Quoted by Mr. HINSDALE from Dr. GILMAN.)

3. The common school system first appeared in Massachusetts. The statute by which it was established is the germ of the American school system. Dr. GILMAN is quoted as thus describing its essential features: "Local responsibility, State oversight, moderate charges or gratuitous instruction; provision for all, and not for the poor alone; and a recognition of three harmonious grades: the primary school, the grammar school and the university."

4. The rapidity of growth is represented as remarkable. "The Massachusetts tree first overspread New England, where it became well-rooted more than a century ago." "When emigration to the West set in, the tide bore the school system along." "Cuttings from the New England tree were thickly planted in the region of the Great Lakes, and in the valley of the Mississippi as far south as the mouths of the Ohio and Missouri; they have been carried over the Rocky Mountains and planted on the Pacific slope." "'Our public schools must be cheap enough for the poorest, and good enough for the best,' has become the distinct aim and purpose of three-fourths of the States and of the people of our Union."

The present situation is thus stated:

"In our Centennial year our common schools constitute a highly complex and differentiated, a vast and powerful system." "In the towns and cities the system has taken on a form especially complex and costly." "The statistics of the system are overwhelming." "What is more, the expenditures are increasing with surprising rapidity." Quoting Mr. FRANCIS ADAMS, Secretary of the National Education League for England, it is said: "During the twenty years expiring in 1870 the population had increased about seventy per cent., and the aggregate amount expended for education had increased to six times the sum raised in 1850." "Well may the evolution of such a system have required more than two hundred years."

In the outset I have to object to the history of the common school as presented by President HINSDALE. From the above sketch, with which he opens his paper, one would be led to believe that the development of the system had been a magnificent and unobstructed progress from the time of the first settlement of New England down to the present day. ●

Unfortunately for Mr. HINSDALE'S argument, and still more unfortunately for our beloved country, his sketch is not history; it is only—rhetoric. So late as fifty years ago the schools of Massachusetts were little better than schools for paupers. Up to within thirty-five or forty years, "cuttings from the Massachusetts tree" were planted, not as schools for the whole people, "cheap enough for the poorest and good enough for the best," but as schools for the poor. If we may judge from the way in which the early school laws were received in Ohio and many other Western States, the common school, instead of being welcomed and kindly cherished in its new home in the West, was treated as a tramp who begs his food from door to door.

Advances in school legislation have been so rapid within the last forty years, that, as Mr. BARNARD says:

"We are already accustomed to speak of the New England system of public instruction as being parts of a well-ordered plan of education established long since and tested by time. * * * It is impossible for the great mass of the rising generation to bear in mind the fact that our present arrangements for education, such as they are in New England, are the creation of active men still on the stage; and that those men themselves, in their early training, had scarcely any other advantage than the unwilling school-boy of Shakes-peare's Seven Ages." *

This is an important point in the discussion of the prevailing education of the day. Its bearing is so obvious that I take some space to review the history of the schools in the New England Colonies, and to set forth as clearly as possible their condition as affected by legislation from the time of the Revolution to within less than a generation ago.

EARLY HISTORY OF EDUCATION IN NEW ENGLAND.

It is to be noted that the early history of education in New England, as honorable as it may be, was not rendered especially illustrious by the establishment and liberal support of elementary schools. It was to the education of the University that the General Court of Massachusetts gave its first attention. To Harvard College, founded only sixteen years after the first settlement of the colony, fell the mites of the poor, the benefactions of the rich, and the appropriations of the State. Nor is this strange. At home they had not been accustomed to the thought of an education of the whole people. The great universities and the endowed grammar schools of England had been created for the education of the clergy and the higher classes. It was natural that the colonists should give their attention to the building up of such kind of schools as they had been accustomed to, that they should aim to perpetuate that learning with which their leaders were familiar. It was not to be expected that their notions of popular education should run much higher than that of the people from whom they had just separated themselves, among whom the opinion prevailed that the education of the masses, beyond a limited ability to read and write, was not necessary for their happiness, nor indeed for the best interests of the State.

It was therefore several years after the General Court of Massachusetts had donated £400 for the building of a "college or school," that the "classic statute" was passed, whereby it was ordered that "in every town of fifty householders" one should be appointed "to teach all such children as shall resort to him to

* Educational Services of Edward Everett, American Journal of Education, Vol. VII. page 325.

write and read," and that "where any town shall increase to the
number of one hundred families or householders, they shall set
up a grammar school,* the master thereof being able to instruct
youth as far as they may be fitted for the University," that is, in
the Latin and Greek languages.†

Let it be observed, that well defined and high qualifications,
were exacted of the master of a "Grammar school," but that for
the lower schools it was only required that "one within the town"
should be appointed "to teach all such children as shall resort to
him to *write and to read.*"

We have not time to trace the history of education from 1647,
the date of the "classic statute" which President GILMAN calls
the "germ of the common school system of New England," down
to the Revolution, a period of about one hundred and thirty years.
Though there were some distinguished schoolmasters in those
days, we can nowhere find that the town "grammar" school
was a very strong or flourishing institution. So far as we can
ascertain, most of the boys who entered college, even from an
early period, were prepared by private tutors, generally ministers
of the gospel.

The lower schools, during this period of a hundred years or
more, are almost lost sight of. It is only in the biographies of
men who lived at the time, that we catch occasional glimpses of
a succession of summer and winter schools; and as they appear
in this way, we find little to commend in them. Descriptions of
them, as they existed in the early part of the present century, are
doubtless as true of those of any preceding period.

At times the common education of the people was at a very
low ebb. Notwithstanding the stringency of the laws requiring

---

*A grammar school was then understood to be a school in which the Latin and Greek
languages were taught. So late as the time of the establishment of the Phillips Academy at
Andover, (1777,) we learn that nothing else was taught in these schools. They were designed
solely for the preparation of boys for college.

†There can be no question that in this very early day these languages were taught better
than they have been at later periods, though at the present time there is a considerable
revival in this respect. In that day Latin at least was taught as a living language. In
Greek the requirements were much less than they now are. The conditions for admission to
Harvard College required by President DUNSTER, for the year 1642, were as follows:

"Whoever shall be able to read Cicero or any other such like classical author at sight,
and correctly, and without assistance to speak and write Latin in prose and verse, and to
inflect exactly the paradigms of Greek nouns and verbs, has a right to expect to be admitted
into the College; and no one may claim admission without these qualifications."

under severe penalty an education so limited, the public records of 1690 and many years thereafter show that "writing was by no means a universal accomplishment, even within the narrow limits of the ability to write one's own name." *

Shortly after the Revolutionary war the condition of affairs was somewhat better, but a quarter of a century thereafter it had become worse than at any previous time.

But it matters very little, in the present inquiry, to know by what measures the colonies sought from time to time to recover the spirit and fulfil the intent of their early laws. It is only necessary for us to know that though the cause of popular education may have moved forward at times, the general tendency was downward. We shall therefore close this review by submitting the testimony of three men as to the general condition of the the schools in New England very little more than a single generation ago. '

The witnesses are men of culture, and "exceptional opportunities for observation." Mr. GEORGE B. EMERSON, a graduate of Harvard in 1817, appointed in 1821 the first master of the English High School in Boston, in 1842 the author of a work entitled "The School Master," which was distributed gratuitously throughout the States of Massachusetts and New York by tens of thousands of copies, an active teacher down to 1855, and to-day one of the most honored men of Boston, is certainly a competent witness. Mr. BARNARD needs no introduction. His name is a familiar word to American teachers, and so with Mr. MANN who is said to have infused that fresh life of which Mr. PEABODY speaks as already "petrifying and petrified."

Mr. EMERSON, in a "Lecture on Education, Legislation and History," delivered before the Lowell Institute, February 16th, 1869, speaking of the period which followed the establishment of the Phillips Academy at Andover, says :

"The common schools and the town grammar schools continued to decline. In the busy world of Massachusetts, men of ability found more profitable employment; and the great truth was not yet discovered that women, as teachers, managers and governors of boys even up to ,manhood, are often gifted at least as highly as men." * * *

---

* Report of 1876, by Hon. B. G. NORTHROP, Secretary of the Board of Education of the State of Connecticut.

"Academies and private schools grew more numerous; sometimes endowed by public-spirited individuals, sometimes by grants of land from the State, often by both, and usually supported in part by fees from the students. In 1834 there were more than nine hundred and fifty of these schools.* Those under the supervision of resolute, judicious men, who knew the value of good teaching and how to secure it, and sometimes others, which by a fortunate accident or a gracious Providence had good teachers, flourished. But the greater number were *very* poor schools; so also were most of the town schools; and the belief and conviction that most of the common schools were wretchedly poor became, except amongst the most ignorant of the teachers themselves and the most benighted of the people, almost universal."

"The laws which we have noticed now became burdensome to the people of Massachusetts. In 1789 a new law was passed which was a wide departure from the original law. Instead of the continuous session of the schools provided for towns of fifty families, a session of six months only was demanded. The number of grammar schools previously required was reduced one-half: that is, one for two hundred families, instead of one hundred as before. It was not long before the Assembly stepped in again to relieve the towns of their burden."

"In 1824, by an act facetiously called 'An ⬛ providing for common schools,' the law of 1789 was repealed; and for all towns of less than five thousand inhabitants, instead of a master of 'good morals, well instructed in the Latin and Greek and English languages,' a teacher or teachers must be provided 'well qualified to instruct youth in orthography, reading, writing, arithmetic, English grammar and geography, and in good behavior.'

The consequences are thus pointed out by Mr. EMERSON :

"This act was the severest blow the common school system ever received, not only because it shut from the poor children of all but a few towns the path which had always laid open to the highest order of education, but because it took away a fixed standard for the qualifications of teachers, and substituted no other in its stead." * * * "The candidate for office of teacher being released from the necessity of an acquaintance with the learned languages, which in most cases implied a certain degree of cultivation and refinement, and amenable to no rule measuring the amount of mere elements, which only were required, was too often found to be lamentably deficient even in them."

"The effect of lowering the standard of instruction in the public schools became to attentive observers every year more apparent. For a time the better qualified teachers continued in the service, but they were gradually supplanted in many places by persons who, from their inferior qualifications were willing to do the work for a lower compensation."

---

* The population of the State, (Massachusetts,) as shown by the census of 1830, was hardly four times as great as the present population of Cleveland.

If further proof of the deterioration of the common schools of Massachusetts be necessary, it will be found in abundance in the earlier reports of HORACE MANN, the first Secretary of the Board of Education of that Commonwealth. Speaking of this deterioration, he says:

"Under this silent but rapid corrosion it recently happened (1836) in one of the most flourishing towns of the State, having a population of more than three thousand persons, that the principal district school actually run down and was not kept for two years." (Page 50, First Annual Report.)

In the biography of Mr. MANN, it is said:

"In Massachusetts the common school system had degenerated in practice from the original theoretic views of the early Pilgrim Fathers. Common and equal opportunities of education for all was the primitive idea of those men who had been so signally made to feel how unequally human rights were shared. The opportunities, unparalleled in the world's history, which the establishment of the Federal Union had opened to all classes of men to obtain wealth, had caused the idea to be nearly lost sight of, and the common schools had been allowed to degenerate into neglected schools for the poorer classes only."

As an instance of the apathy of the people in regard to common schools, we may quote still further from the Life of HORACE MANN an account of a Convention held in the city of Salem in 1837, pages 91 and 92:

"One gentleman, who made one of the first speeches, questioned the expediency of endeavoring to get the educated classes to patronize public schools. He spoke, he said, in the interest of mothers who preferred private schools for their children; and he believed the reasons that they had for this would always prevail; they would have their children grow up in intimacies with those of their own class."

In his diary, and in numerous letters to Mr. COMBE, Mr. MANN presents for nearly every town he visited the same dark picture. Everywhere he met a degree of apathy or open opposition sufficient to discourage any one who had not within him the spirit of a hero.

The early history of education in the State of Connecticut was almost identical with that of Massachusetts. In 1650, three years after its enactment by the Court of Massachusetts, the "classic statute" was adopted by the State of Connecticut in almost the

same, if not the very words of the original. Step by step these
two States kept pace with each other in almost steady retro-
gression till after the Revolution. Shortly after the war had
closed, Connecticut became possessed of a considerable school
fund from the sale of public lands in the Western Reserve, and
relying exclusively upon this for the support of her schools, she
began to fall behind her sister State, or I should say rather to
pass her in the steep descent. In his Centennial Report already
referred to, Mr. NORTHROP says:

"The multiplication until about 1840 of academies and of select schools,
more or less permanent, for teaching branches now universally taught in the
public schools, gives clear indication of the inferiority and the unsatisfactory
condition of the common schools."

Mr. BARNARD, in his Journal of Education, page 154, vol. V.,
speaking of education in Connecticut, says:

"Private schools not only for the higher branches of an English education,
and for preparation for business or college, but for the primary studies, were
established in every town and society and liberally supported, not only by the
rich and educated, but by many who could only afford to do so by making
large sacrifices of comforts and almost the necessaries of life, rather than to
starve the intellect and impoverish the hearts of their children. Taxation for
school purposes had not only ceased to be the cheerful habit of the people,
but was regarded as something foreign and anti-democratic. The supervision
of the schools had become in most societies a mere formality, and the system
seemed struck with paralysis."

In the History of Education in RHODE ISLAND, by THOMAS
WENTWORTH HIGGINSON, it is said:

"The public school system of this State dates back, as distinctly as can be
the case with any institution, to the labors of one man."

JOHN HOWLAND, successively a barber, a soldier under
WASHINGTON, Treasurer of the first Savings Bank in Providence, President of the Rhode Island Historical Society, and a
member of the Mechanics' Association in 1789, began to work
for the establishment of a common school system through the
agency of the Association last named. His efforts were partially
successful. A law establishing a common school system was
enacted, but except in the city of Providence, the law met with
the most determined opposition throughout the State; the whole

measure was virtually defeated by non-enforcement, and the law itself was repealed at the February session, 1803.*

On page 23, Mr. HIGGINSON says:

"For twenty-five years after the defeat of JOHN HOWLAND'S enterprise, Rhode Island had no public school system even on paper."

In 1828 a "school act" was finally passed, and the machinery of the common school system was slowly put in motion. How tardy were the blessings which had been expected may be judged by remarks made in the State Assembly of 1843, by Mr. UPDIKE, on the introduction of a bill "to provide for ascertaining the condition of the public schools in this State," etc. Mr. UPDIKE stated boldly that

"The free school system, as it existed, was not a blessing to the State, except in the city, of Providence, and possibly in a few other towns where a similar course was pursued. * * * Our teachers come from abroad, are employed without producing evidence either of moral character or their fitness to teach, remain in the schools two or three months, and within twenty-four hours of the close of the month are gone to parts unknown."

At the next session of the Assembly, in 1845, Mr. UPDIKE said:

"There is a wide-spread dissatisfaction with the schools as they are; with the inefficient manner in which the system is administered; with the shortness of time for which the schools are kept,—although they are quite long enough, unless they can be kept by better teachers," etc., etc.

What the causes of this neglect of the primary schools may have been, it does not concern us to inquire at any length; but the mention of one at least may not be without service. The early settlers brought to America the class distinctions which existed in the mother country.† The interests of those who looked to a university education as essential for their boys, were soon separated from the interests of the lower classes, especially in the matter of education. The schools for the two classes, except for children under seven or eight years of age, were not

* History of the Public School System of Rhode Island, by THOMAS WENTWORTH HIGGINSON, pp. 13-24.

† The Catalogue of Yale College was not arranged alphabetically, but in order of rank, even down to 1773, only two years before the breaking out of the Revolutionary War.

the same. The lower schools were in consequence neglected by those whose care was essential to their efficiency—in fact their very life. In this day when the opinion appears to be growing that the education of the laboring man should be confined to the narrow limits of the "three R's," it may be of service to call to mind that in America at least it is impossible to provide separately for the education of people of limited means, and those of the wealthier classes. The effort at this period of which we speak as of later periods, was in vain. The education of both has always suffered in common in this country. Especially has the influence of the separation been fatal to the education of the poor. As soon as the interest and patronage of the better educated classes is withdrawn from the public schools, they must go down.* The poor will not accept education as a gratuity from the rich, unless provision be made for all alike. The common schools cannot be made efficient unless it is to the personal interest of the educated classes to make them so. In public education every class distinction must be obliterated save one and that distinction is between the educated and the ignorant.

Testimony similar to, and in support of that which I have already submitted, might be swelled to volumes. The enactments of Legislatures, and the reports of committees almost without number, are full of evidence that the common school system, in the first quarter or half of the present century, was not in New England regarded as a system "cheap enough for the poorest, and good enough for the best," but that, as a system for the education of the whole people, it had died of neglect and starvation in its mother's arms. †

I have said that "cuttings from this New England tree" were planted in other States as schools for the poor; that they were not received "without opposition," as President GILMAN states;

---

* For evidence of this fact the reader is referred to the earlier Reports of HORACE MANN, to the discussions in the Proceedings of the Western College of Teachers, Vols. I and II, published 1835 and 1836; to the Reports of the Superintendents of Schools for the States of Pennsylvania and New York; to the experience of Virginia and every other Southern State, as shown in letters, speeches and public documents too numerous for me to note.

† "The common school idea may have worked independently from other centers; * * * but if Virginia be the mother of States and of statesmen, Massachusetts is the mother of schools." (Mr. HINSDALE's Address, page 16.)

but that almost up to the time of the late Rebellion they met with opposition bitter and protracted wherever the effort was made to domesticate them in new soil.

As an introduction to evidence on this point, I find nothing better than an extract from a speech of Hon. JAMES A. GAR-FIELD, who till within a few months ago had his home under the shadow of Hiram College, and who was a highly respected predecessor of Mr. HINSDALE as the head of that institution.

While the Bill for the Establishment of a Bureau of Education was pending in the House of Representatives, June 8th, 1876, Mr. GARFIELD, who had introduced the bill said:

"Gentlemen tell us there is no need of this bill; the States are doing well enough now. Do they know through what a struggle every State has come up that has secured a good system of common schools? Let me illustrate this by the example of Pennsylvania. Notwithstanding the early declaration of WILLIAM PENN: 'That which makes a good Constitution must keep it, namely, men of wisdom and virtue—qualities that because they descend not with wordly inheritance must be carefully propagated by a virtuous education of youth, for which spare no cost, for by such parsimony all that is saved is lost;' notwithstanding that wise master-builder incorporated this sentiment in his 'frame-work of government,' and made it the duty of the Governor and Council 'to establish and support public schools;' nothwithstanding BENJA-MIN FRANKLIN, from the first hour he became a citizen of Pennsylvania, inculcated the value of useful knowledge to every human being in every walk of life, and by his personal and pecuniary effort did establish schools and a college for Philadelphia; notwithstanding the Constitution of Pennsylvania made it obligatory upon the Legislature to foster the education of the citizens; notwithstanding all this, it was not until 1833-'34 that a system of common schools, supported in part by taxation of property of the State for the common benefit of all children of the State, was established by law; and although the law was passed by an almost unanimous vote of both branches of the Legis-lature, so forcign was the idea of public schools to the habits of the people, so odious was the idea of taxation for this purpose, that even the poor who were to be specially benefited were so deluded by political demagogues as to clamor for its repeal."

I would like to quote at length Mr. GARFIELD's eloquent tribute to THADDEUS STEVENS, then a member of the House, for the noble stand which he had taken in behalf of this law; but lack of space forbids us to do more than give a brief extract relating to the proceedings of the State Legislature at its session held in 1835:

"Many members who had voted for the law had lost their nominations, and others although nominated lost their election. Some were weak enough to pledge themselves to a repeal of the law; and in the session of 1835 there was an almost certain prospect of its repeal, and the adoption in its place of an odious and limited provision for educating the children of the poor by themselves."

From the fact that the law was finally sustained, it might be inferred that the common school system was at length established without condition or danger of repeal, and that its blessings were thenceforward to be enjoyed by the children of the rich and poor alike. Three years thereafter it was submitted to the vote of the districts whether they should accept the provisions of the law or not; and although it was adopted by all without exception, in 1853, nearly twenty years afterward, the Superintendent of Instruction, ANDREW G. CURTIN, reported:

"That the common school system had sadly disappointed the expectations of its friends. The State appropriation being received, in many districts no schools were opened, no teachers employed; the money was applied to the repair of township roads, or transferred to the pockets of the directors themselves as compensation for their official services; in others, schools were established that were a mere burlesque on the cause of popular education; many of the school-houses were fitter subjects for the consideration of grand juries than for the purposes of their dedications. All who could afford it carefully withheld their children from the common schools; in short, the system of public instruction was rapidly becoming a by-word and reproach to the Commonwealth."

EDUCATION IN OHIO.

Let us take a more particular view of common school education in our own State. We shall find that it was no exception to the general rule.

Though it was decreed in 1785 that one thirty-sixth part of the public lands of the State should be reserved for the maintenance of public schools within the State; though the great Ordinance of 1787 proclaimed that religion, morals and knowledge being essential to good government, schools and the means of education should forever be encouraged; though the Constitution of the State, adopted 1802, proclaimed that the means of instruction should be forever encouraged by legislative provision; though taxes had been levied for school purposes for many years; though funds were accumulating by the sale of school lands and from other sources, Mr. COGGESHALL, in his "History of the Common Schools of Ohio," says: "There were no public schools in Ohio, in 1837," that is, thirty-five years after the admission of the Territory to the rank and dignity of a State. (Barnard's American Journal of Education, Vol. VI., p. 86.)

Again, Mr. COGGESHALL, in a sketch of the Life of SAMUEL LEWIS, the first Superintendent of the schools of the State, says :

"He began his work in the spring of 1837. * * * He found that, except in Cincinnati, there were no schools in the State practically open alike to rich and poor." Barnard's Journal, etc., Vol. V., p. 729.

In 1845, eight years after the first effectual steps towards the establishment of the common school, the first Teachers' Institute conducted in Ohio was held in Sandusky by SALEM TOWN of New York, and M. F. COWDERY and A. D. LORD of this State. Mr. COGGESHALL says of this Institute:

"It was the result however of local rather than general interest; but that a general interest in such opportunities for teachers was then imperatively demanded, may be inferred from the fact that in many districts directors forbade the teaching of any branches but reading, writing and arithmetic, and that certificates were given to teachers who were pedagogues only because school-keeping was easier for their muscular system than chopping wood." (Barnard's Journal, Vol. VI., p. 90.)

Let us look into the volumes of "Transactions of the Literary Institute and Western College of Professional Teachers" which were published from 1834 to 1840. But before citing some of the evidence which is to be found in these records, it may be well to glance at a list of the committees of the association in which we shall find striking proof of the low standing of those who were then engaged in the instruction of the children of the people. Out of twenty-four officers of State sections named on page 14, Vol. I., nearly one-half were private school-masters, and most of the others were lawyers, doctors or clergymen, not one, so far as I can ascertain, was a teacher of the common schools.

The titles of addresses pertaining to the lower schools were such as the following : "Report on the Best Method of Establishing and Forming Common Schools in the West," by SAMUEL LEWIS; "On Elevating Public School Teachers," by Dr. JOSEPH

RAY, etc., etc.   A few lines from President MONTGOMERY's Essay
"On the Importance of Education," Vol. III., page 153, will show
the spirit of many of the papers which were read before the
College:

"Failing in trade, bankrupt in business, even the spendthrift, all, every one,
from the highest to the lowest unsuccessful in his occupation, calculated to
repair his fortune in the school-master.   Nay, the very sot reckoned on
replenishing the intoxicating cup with the gleanings of a country school."

Again, in an eloquent address at the close of the session of
1836, the Rev. ALEXANDER CAMPBELL, referring to his experience
as a teacher about fifteen years before, said:

"Books without philosophy, and teachers without science or art, if they
were only at a low price, seemed to have the universal sway."   Vol. III.,
page 254.

But it is especially in a discussion on the examination of teachers, held at the previous session, that we find the most direct
and explicit testimony.   During the discussion, EDWARD D.
MANSFIELD said:

"As an *examiner* of common schools, I have carefully examined their statistics, and inquired into the manner in which they have been conducted.   The
result of my investigation is melancholy.   It has led me to the painful conclusion that the college of the people, at present, furnishes but little of what the
people ought to know.

"I have examined within the last twelve months, one hundred and fifty
applicants for the office of teacher.   The requirements of the law are the
mere rudiments of reading, writing and arithmetic; yet, sir, upon these simple
matters how many do we find deficient! and are yet compelled to pass them
in some way, or deprive the country of its teachers.   In many instances the
applicant requests us not to examine him very closely, for he has no scholars
beyond the Rule of Three! and consequently had no practice.   There is
scarcely one teacher in ten in the *country*, who has *thoroughly studied* more
than the ground rules of this science.   They are generally deficient in what a
teacher ought to know best—the *reasons of things*.   It will do for a judge to
decide without *reasons;* but a teacher cannot *teach* without showing the
reasons of rules.   *Repetition* is not *teaching*.   Nor is this all; the number of
those who cannot read with proper emphasis and pronunciation; or reading,
do not understand what they read—is lamentable."   (Transactions of College
of Teachers, 1835, Vol. II., p. 170.)

The following are the remarks of Judge LOOKER on the same occasion :

"These two things, sir, the want of a sufficient 'support for the teachers, and the inefficiency of the present modes of examining them, are altogether inadequate to the wants of the rising generation; and, sir, in my opinion, they are an injury to our country rather than a benefit; they are worse than nothing. * * * I have spent twenty years of my life in teaching, and have had every opportunity of witnessing the low condition of our schools." (Ibid, p. 167.)

Speaking of the incompetency of teachers, Judge LOOKER said :

"The compensation is so small as to prevent competent men from engaging in this business.* . . . Why, sir, I have seen those who could neither read to be understood by others nor themselves, employed to give instruction to our children. This ought not to be. Every one will cry out against it; but why do they not provide the remedy?" (Ibid, p. 166.)

Said one gentleman :

"I am called on to examine candidates for school teachers who are often destitute of the very elements of education. A knowledge even of the multiplication table is not always to he procured; as for grammar and spelling, these are even proud accomplishments, and we are glad to secure them." (Ibid, p. 164.)

Were such things said to-day in our educational conventions, as were then declared to be generally true over the greater part of the State, there would be an indignant protest from town and city, because, of them, at least, they would be untrue. But on that and similar occasions not a voice was heard in behalf of the common schools. The testimony thus given against them was recognized as being too true.

In the debates of the Legislature, shortly after, we hear the same cry raised. At the session of 1838, Judge JOHNSON spoke as follows :

"We are in the habit of calling ourselves the most enlightened, intelligent people on earth; but after the developments of this evening respecting Prussia, and even Russia, can we pretend that there is any good foundation for this habitual self-applause? * * * But what is, what has been, the state of common school education among us? I well remember when I used to wade three miles.

* It was just about what could be earned by working men on the farm, and less than could be earned by a respectable mechanic, and even this was thought to be good pay.

over my little knees in snow, to the district school. The population was sparse
and poor. Our school-house was built of logs, without glass windows, but with
plenty of inlets between the logs for air and light. * * * Our teacher was a
good man and taught all he knew. But his attainments were not great. As
to astronomy, he never had an idea but that the earth was as flat as the plate
on which he ate his breakfast; and as to mathematics, the difference between
the numerator and denominator of a vulgar fraction, was a mystery of science
altogether beyond his depth."

If we turn to School Reports, which President HINSDALE
speaks of as self-laudatory, we meet with the same account of the
condition of the common schools. SAMUEL GALLOWAY, Secretary
of State, and *ex-officio* Superintendent of Common Schools, said
in his annual report for 1845:

"It is impossible even to conjecture what is the number or condition
of the school houses in Ohio: but it is more than probable that a faithful
description would embrace a grotesque scenery of broken benches, rock-
ing slabs, broken sashes, absent panes, gaping walls, yawning roofs, and
floors bowing without furniture, forcibly suggesting Falstaff's account of his
regiment: 'No eye hath seen such scare-crows. There's but a shirt and a half
in all my company, and the half-shirt is but two napkins tacked together, and
thrown over the shoulders like a herald's coat without sleeves.' The contrast,
in reference to all other items, would be as unfavorable to us, as in that which
has been instituted." * * *

"Although education holds an acknowledged superiority, by the profession
of our people, and in intrinsic merit is unrivaled by any competitor, yet, it has
been exiled from an honorable companionship in the family of State interests,
and has been thrown out like a poor, despised foundling, half-clad and half-
fed, to beg for protection." (Doc. No. 33—Report of the Secretary of State
on Condition of Common Schools, pp. 502, 503.)

And again in the same document, speaking of the qualifications
of teachers, Mr. GALLOWAY says:

"Elevated and commanding as the talents and attainments of a teacher
ought to be, one obtains license to teach orthography, who replied to the
question 'Spell ocean,' that there were two ways of spelling it, 'otion and
oshion;' another who spelled ' philosophy,' 'filosefey,' and another who spelled
the common word 'earthly,' 'erthley.' Upon others were bestowed the
honor of teacher of arithmetic: one of whom could not tell how many cwt.
were in a ton; another who was ignorant of the multiplication table, and
another who could not tell the cost of nine cords of wood at $1.37½ per cord.
Another was licensed to teach geography who, in reply to the question, ' How
is Virginia bounded?' answered, ' By Tennessee on the north and Maryland
on the east.' These are but a few of many specimens communicated by friends

of education as evidences of the kind and amount of qualifications tolerated in some sections of our country." (Ibid, p. 511.)

But evidence in regard to the state of common schools in Ohio only a few years ago may be drawn from other sources than Examining boards, State Legislators and Superintendents of education. We have the the testimony of the pulpit, which is as direct and pointed as any that we have already submitted. In the November number of the Ohio School Journal, published in 1846, we find extracts from a sermon preached by the Rev. LEVERITT HULL at Sandusky, during the session of the first Teachers' Institute held in this State, to which we have already referred. He said :

"It is the sober conviction of men well qualified to judge, that the entire system of select and high-schools* and academies, has been and is still greatly defective, and never will accomplish what we so much desire. Their principal defects are these : in them, the first principles of a practical, sound and thorough education are passed over or neglected. They rear a superstructure without a foundation. But their great defect is, by their existence, the interests of district schools have been utterly laid waste, and the mass of the population are left untutored and untamed. The general impression has been, any body can teach a common school, because it *is common,* and no one expected that the children who attend the district school could learn anything but evil. Hence every district must have its select school, and no teacher qualified to teach, would enter a district school. All who had money, and cared for their children, or for the interests of education, have fostered the academy or select school."

We have also the testimony of teachers themselves. The following is taken from Vol. III. of the "Ohio School Journal," published in 1849, under the editorship of Dr. A. D. LORD, who for more than a quarter of a century was identified with every great educational movement in this State. Dr. LORD thus introduces the article from which we make a short extract :

"We copy from the 'Ohio Eagle' the following severe, but just and truthful remarks on the condition of common schools in our towns and villages. They are from the pen of an intelligent and faithful teacher of long experience and much observation:

* * * 'In the villages and towns there is a progressive deterioration, according to the numbers of population, till, in places of from three to five

---

*He does not speak here of public high schools, for there were none at that date.

thousand inhabitants, the schools are found to have reached a maximum of degradation, so that human ingenuity could not possible render them more superlatively contemptible. Hence our towns, and especially the larger ones, instead of being centers of illumination, are points at which all the scattered *rays* of the intellectual *darkness* which pervades the surrounding community are concentrated in foci of the intensest blackness.'"

PUBLIC SCHOOLS OF VARIOUS STATES FROM 1853 TO 1858.

We have seen that the "cuttings from the New England tree," which were "thickly planted by the Great Lakes and in the Valley of the Mississippi as far south," etc., were only cuttings from the stunted shrub which was to be found at the time in the oldest of the North-eastern States. Let us next see what these cuttings were, and how they grew in other States down to the time of the civil war, when another kind of tree was planted in a soil that had been enriched by the best blood of a noble people, a tree under which poor and rich alike will gather for protection, and whose leaves shall be for the healing of the nation.

In the report of the Superintendent of Education of ALABAMA it is said:

"The melancholy reflection still obtrudes itself that three-fourths of the youth of the state have hitherto gone without instruction entirely, or have been crowded into miserable apologies of school houses, without furniture or apparatus deserving the name, and still oftener, without competent teachers." * * * "Owls and bats are still employed to teach young eagles how to fly, because they will work cheap."

ARKANSAS, so far as free school education is concerned, seems to be a universal blank. In the "Education Year-book" of 1857, we find a report of only forty schools in the state, with but thirty-one teachers, with an aggregate of more than $100,000, current expenses. In the following year, the Commissioner of Common Schools is reported to have said:

"Considering the almost entire failure successfully to organize and establish Common Schools in Arkansas, at present, I am inclined to believe that the interests of education would in the end, be promoted by a suspension of the sale of the public lands."

CALIFORNIA. The Superintendent says:

"*We have no free school system.* It is true that cities are empowered, under certain restrictions, to raise means, and to a certain extent, to maintain free schools. The counties may or may not levy a limited tax to maintain schools, but in some densely settled counties, no tax whatever has been levied for school purposes."

CONNECTICUT. Under the able superintendency of JOHN D. PHILBRICK, this state is treated of as hopeful, but when we learn that the average wages of female teachers left them but $1.75 per week, after their board of $2,50 was paid, we may readily imagine that the service they performed could not have been of a very high grade. "Labor in the kitchen was, all things considered, more remunerative, and indeed in the rural districts of that state, quite as respectable."

LOUISIANA. So late as 1853, many directors, whose duty it was under the law to examine teachers, signed orders upon the treasury by making their "marks." In the "Education Year-book" of 1858, it is said,

"For reasons thus indicated, the school system of Louisiana can scarcely be said to be in successful operation. The Governor speaks of it as 'almost a failure.' The schools of one or two parishes in New Orleans were said to be good."

DELAWARE. The record of the "Education Year-book" is, that this State "has a school system organized wholly upon the plan ' of free tuition for all the pupils, and a school within the reach of every family," but the report of the Superintendent for the year 1855 represents the schools as in a "deplorable state." I have neither space nor time even to summarize his specification of faults, the greatest of which is gross ignorance among teachers themselves.

GEORGIA. In 1854, this State distributed through her magistrates, $23,000, for the education of *indigent children.* This is enough from which to estimate the educational advantages of the poor whites of Georgia.

ILLINOIS. The average wages of male teachers, was $25 per month, and of females, $12. There were over 4,000 schools in the State and the amount paid for teachers' wages in 79 counties, is reported to be $308,385, less than $4,000 per county, and less than $80 per school.

INDIANA. The "Education Year-book," of 1858, says: "The cause of free schools is most emphatically in its infancy there," and the Superintendent of Public Instruction speaks of the schools as in a "transition state" but expresses high hopes of the future though the number who could not *read* or *write* had, from 1840 to 1850, mounted up from 38,000 to 75,000, or nearly 100 per cent., while the population had increased but 50 per cent. in the same time.

KENTUCKY is well known to have had the most efficient system of schools among the Southern States, but measured by any standard you please, they must have been inferior to those of the three States lying on the other side of the Ohio River. Her school officers have never confessed their inferiority, but having spent three months in 1853 in traveling through the central and western parts of the State, my own personal observation enables me to say, that outside of the city of Louisville, there were no public schools which were patronized by people who could afford to send to any other.

In 1856, the NEW ENGLAND schools had begun to feel something of the impulse which HORACE MANN had sought to give the schools of Massachusetts, but which was resisted by the school-master as long as he could resist—how long and how successfully can be ascertained by reference to the reports of the school visitors of the city of Boston, in 1845, and the replies thereto which the masters were goaded to make. But though the schools had possibly begun to feel the shock, the States themselves had done comparatively little for their better organization and management so late even as 1856. It is true that valuable agencies, such as Normal Schools, Teachers' Institutes, etc., had been set to work, but their influence had not been felt to any considerable degree, except in a few leading cities and in the more intelligent districts which stood readiest to avail themselves of the advantages of the times.

VIRGINIA. In this State, nine counties and two towns had adopted free schools, that is, schools for rich and poor alike. In 117 counties and two towns, there were pauper schools for children of the indigent. If we need again that attention should be be directed to the consequences of this separate education of the poor and rich, we have it already stated in the speech of C. G. MEMMINGER, Esq., on the occasion of inaugurating the common school system at Charleston, South Carolina, July 4th, 1856. This extract will serve also to inform us as to the condition of popular education at the same time in

SOUTH CAROLINA. He says:

"The fund," that is, for public education, "was small, and was entirely absorbed by the preferred class," (the poor.) "The rich were thus excluded, and the benefit being confined to the poor, the schools degenerated into pauper schools, and pupils and teachers descended to the grade at which they are now found throughout the State. No one, unless urged by necessity, would accept an education which could only be granted as a charity. The middling classes of society were unwilling to stigmatize themselves by a declaration of pauperism, and the result has been here, as everywhere else, that schools for the poor have signally failed in the main objects for which they were instituted."   *   *

"Try the same experiment with any other educational institution, let it be required that no young man shall find entrance into the South Carolina College, but upon the declaration that his parents are unable to educate him. Such a regulation would be fatal to its existence—its whole tone and character would be destroyed ; and if enough of those who could receive such a bounty ·could be found to secure the continuance of the college, they would soon lose consideration in the community, and professors and students would descend by the same steps which the free schools of the State have taken."

PURPOSES OF THE FOREGOING HISTORICAL SKETCH.

The foregoing sketch of the history of the common school system, as well as the statements of many witnesses as to the actual condition of the schools up to a very recent date, are submitted to show,

First, how inaccurate is the historical sketch with which President HINSDALE opens his paper. To establish this, however, would be of very little importance; but by showing that he is in error when he says "we yield to none in our devotion to popular elementary instruction;" that his statement is exactly contrary to fact when he says, in the language of Dr. GILMAN, "every new State adopts it (the common school system) without hesitation;" and that instead of being the "growth of two hundred years," the present system, in all its essential features, is hardly fifty years old, we go very far toward weakening confidence in every state

3

ment which he makes. If he errs so greatly in regard to well-known historical facts, what blunder is he not likely to make when he confesses that he has only "meagre," "vague" and "uncertain" data to rely upon ?

Second. I desire to show that the faults of the schools of our times are owing in good part to the fact that the great majority of teachers of the present day are the pupils of the teachers and schools, such as have been described in the preceding pages.

Third. My purpose is to show that the enormous increase of expenditures to which Mr. HINSDALE refers is the necessary result of the rapid improvement which has been made in the physical apparatus of education, and more than all else to a growing feeling on the part of the people that they need educators for their children, not mere day laborers. The wages of a sculptor are higher than those of a quarryman.

But we are not yet through with this branch of our subject. Our brief historical sketch is an account of the gradual sinking of the common school education until it had, as Mr. MANN says, " been nearly lost sight of."   The testimony so far has related to the general condition of education at successive periods one, two and three generations ago, rather than to the working of the schools themselves ; and our attention has been directed to the moral and literary qualifications, or more appropriately disqualifi- cations of the schoolmaster, and not to the quality of his teaching. One would suppose this to be enough, for if the schoolmaster be uneducated, how can he be an educator ? "As is the teacher, so is the school." But we have evidence still more direct. We have the testimony of those who went to school a few years after the Revolution, and in the early days of the present century ; testimony in which we find a pretty full account of the better (?) work which was done at those periods. But inasmuch as it is intended to rebut the evidence of Dr. PEABODY, and to disprove the avowals of President HINSDALE, it is no more than right that we should place their testimony before the reader.

Let us then turn to the presentation of the case as made by our critics.

PRESIDENT HINSDALE QUESTIONS WHETHER WE ARE MAKING REAL EDUCATIONAL PROGRESS.

I quote the first paragraph in which MR. HINSDALE turns to question the educational progress of the day:

"In view of the foregoing facts, what wonder that we should contemplate this great school system with a good deal of complacency! What wonder that we should conclude that, in the best sense of the word, we are making rapid educational progress! With few exceptions, the teachers and other school functionaries say we are, and the great public acquiesces with the schoolmasters. With the exception of a few scarcely audible voices to the contrary, there is a want of either the inclination or the courage to say nay."

"The arguments urged to prove real progress in great degree are, increase in the number, and improvement in kind of school houses, more and better school apparatus and furniture, more teachers and higher wages. * * * These premises do not legitimate the conclusions. * * * The most important conditions of education are not an excellent physical apparatus; they are competent and devoted teachers and eager pupils.

"But the eulogists of the popular system *.* * claim a great improvement in teachers, books and methods. Generally they pass lightly over the qualities of the teacher, * * * but they make up for their reticence on this point by the stress they place on books and methods." "The part that the new methods play in the current theories of education is something wonderful," etc., etc.

Here is the entire paragraph in which President HINSDALE puts the main question:

"Let us then boldly ask: Is the quality of our common school education improving? Be it noted, the question is not whether our school system has been greatly extended, whether more children enjoy its benefits, whether it costs more money, whether there are more and more learned teachers, or whether the physical apparatus has been greatly improved—no one thinks of denying these propositions. Nor is it whether the common school pupil of to-day is taught more things than the common school pupil of fifty or a hundred years ago, for that question is as undeniable as the others. But the question is this: Whether we read and write, spell and cipher better than our ancestors one, two or three generations ago."

The difficulties of the inquiry are recognized as follows:

"At the outset we encounter this difficulty: to find a common standard of measure. There are but two methods of procedure. One is by means of historical testimony, written or traditional, to determine the attainments of former generations of pupils, and then to compare them with the attainments of this generation. Such testimony, especially in a written form, is meagre, not to speak of its vagueness and uncertainty. The other method is to take the opinions of those yet living who had, either by experience or tradition, immediate knowledge of the instruction formerly given in the schools. * * * But because the inquiry is difficult we should not shrink from it; rather, using such methods as we have, let us essay the task."

DIRECT EVIDENCE IMPOSSIBLE.

Before hearing the testimony which Mr. HINSDALE submits as a warrant for raising the doubts which he has here so boldly expressed, it may be well to speak of the general nature of the evidence which is within our reach. By way at once of argument and illustration, we may refer to one of the branches in which Mr. HINSDALE claims a deterioration of our common school edu-tion. For instance:

Take the matter of spelling. What evidence has MR. HINSDALE found to prove the inferiorty of our common school education in this respect? He says that he has given twenty years to the study of this subject. Would he not have found some direct and reliable testimony on this point if it were to be had? But he offers none. Exemplifying the old adage, which we shall not quote, he only asks the question, "Whether we do spell better," etc. We have found some testimony for him on this point but, as we shall see, it is not evidence. For instance :

We can find plenty of men, of scholarship and learning, who will tell us that they *think* that spelling in the schools has dete-riorated within the present generation ; but, twenty years ago, the Rev. HEMAN HUMPHREY said the same thing and somewhere about twenty years before that, HORACE MANN, WILLIAM B. FOWLE and others expressed opinions to like effect, as to the degeneracy of the schools in this important branch of learning. Finally we come to NOAH WEBSTER himself, who said :

"The introduction of my spelling-book, first published in 1783, produced a great change in the department of spelling, and from the information I can gain, spelling was taught with more care and accuracy for twenty or more years after that period, than it has been since the introduction of multiplied books and studies."

Thus we are carried back to within thirty years of the publica-tion of Johnson's Dictionary, the first standard of English orthog-raphy.

But in a serious inquiry as to the quality of our common school education, what is such guess-work worth? Is it possible that spelling has been becoming worse and worse since within twenty-five years of the very origin of spelling-books? If it has, so much the worse for the spelling-books and so much the worse for the way spelling has been taught in the schools of the past.

It will be observed that each individual referred to only thinks that there had been deterioration in spelling. Not one feels so confident as to say flatly that it is so. Now is it not altogether probable that the impression among adults that there are more poor spellers among the young than there were when they were young themselves, has grown upon them as they have become more critical? When they were faulty spellers themselves they did not see the defect in others, but as they have improved by practice, they begin to forget the mistakes of their youth. How unreliable such vague impressions are, especially regarding things near and remote either in space or time, is well pointed out by HERBERT SPENCER, in his "Study of Sociology."

Such is the only direct evidence we can get at, but "I think," and "from the information I can gain," are not admissable as evidence, unless the ground of the opinion or the information itself is laid before the court. The only direct evidence which could be of any worth would have to be obtained in some such way as this:

If the spelling of adults were in question, we should have to compare the spelling of large numbers of people of different classes now living, with the spelling of a like number of people in the same walks of life, one, two or three generations ago, Those of to-day would have to be selected from districts widely separated from each other, and so would those of the past. It would not do to take a hundred or two, say from Providence, R. I., only, and compare their orthography with that of their ancestors a hundred years before, for Providence may be up to the general standard of to-day, but might not have been then.

But it is not whether we spell better than our ancestors that concerns us in this inquiry, for that would afford us no test of the quality of the instruction now given in the best graded schools.

The adults of 1877 were educated, the most of them at least, in schools as they were taught by a former race of school masters.* No, the comparison would have to be between the work of boys and girls of to-day, and that of corresponding classes of boys and girls fifty or a hundred years ago. Cities in different parts of the country, and country towns where graded schools now exist, would have to be drawn upon for the manuscripts of children of corresponding ages in this and former days and the number of misspellings in each counted. It is only by such a spelling-match of generations that the improvement or deterioration of our schools in this branch, could be established to the satisfaction of any tribunal that had respect for its own reputation.

As we have said, direct evidence is impossible, and the very ground for this statement is good proof that the pupils in the graded schools of the Western Reserve, at least, are, at the same ages better practical spellers than those of the schools which Dr. Peabody says "did more for their pupils than is done now." The impossibility of which we speak, arises not from the fact that such manuscripts have not been preserved, but from the fact that there never were any to preserve, certainly none in such quantity as to justify any conclusion as to the comparative merits of the schools of to-day and the schools of the past.

The truth is that the boy of a generation or two ago, even in the best of schools, except, it might be, one in a thousand, did no writing except a few lines in his copy book, and copy one or two sums every day or two in his arithmetic manuscript. We have good reasons to believe that more manuscript work, and hence more spelling was done last year in the city of Cleveland than was done in Boston during the entire first forty years of the present century.

---

* By way of illustrating the very queer mistakes which are often made by men of more than ordinary culture when they come to speak of school education, I may quote from a letter recently received from the Hon. E. E. WHITE, President of Purdue University, whose distinguished career as an educator in this State is well known to us all. Mr. WHITE says :

"A few years since I heard a Cleveland editor, now deceased, lament the decline in spelling, and he sharply charged the result to modern methods of teaching spelling, and to a general neglect of the subject in the schools. He stated, as an illustration, that he received lawyer's briefs and political speeches, the spelling of which was very discreditable. He was taken back and puzzled when I asked him, at the close of the lecture, if most of these briefs and speeches were not written by men forty years of age and upwards. He reluctantly admitted they were, and of course thereby admitted that the spelling was the result of former teaching or neglect. This was nearly twenty years ago.

This may be circumstantial evidence, based on "grounds of theory," if you like, Mr. President, but in the estimate of men of practical common sense it will go far to prove that the pupils in our schools are now taught the art of spelling to better advantage than in the schools of the past. To teach spelling practically, there is no way so effective as that of frequent practice in writing with constant correction of errors in orthography.

From the fact that in addition to the oral spelling, which we do not neglect, we require also the daily writing at dictation of long spelling lessons, and the careful preparation of a great number of papers in answer to written and printed questions, which are examined by teachers, and then re-written and corrected by the pupils, no doubt can be entertained that our children have ten, nay fifty times more practice in spelling than they did even in the halcyon days of NOAH WEBSTER, to say nothing of the fact that they are taught by the only method that can make good spellers ; —and if an examination, such as I have indicated could be had, there is no doubt that the boys and girls in our schools would spell the common vocabulary better than those who have occupied their places at the school desk at any previous period in the history of American education.

Before submitting testimony as to work which was really done in the schools of the earlier days of the Republic, and down to times which are only a little beyond the recollection of the older pupils now in our schools, let us glance at the evidence upon which Mr. HINSDALE depends to prove the inferiority of our elementary instruction.

. In the first place, our attention is directed to the doubts of a "considerable number of people who do not see that what the schoolmasters tell them is true." Mr. HINSDALE continues:

"But the other day a lady, forming one of a company where this question was raised—a lady of much more than ordinary intelligence and character— said: "All I can say about it is, my children are not so far along with their studies as I was with mine at their ages." A man has only to keep his ears open, at most, to provoke frequent conversations on this subject, to learn that the class who will give similar testimony is a large and respectable one. In fact, while it is the understanding that we have been making great advances in the quality of our common education, and while it takes some courage to say nay, there is unexpressed a large amount of incredulity on this point, and a widespread dissatisfaction with the results of the popular system. Reference is here made chiefly to intelligent persons outside the teaching profession who do not make especial pretensions to culture. These persons may be wrong,. but they are entitled to be heard."

" In the second place, there is a class of highly-cultured men, some of them educators, who do not join in the paeans to the prevalent system. *On the contrary, they say the present results are inferior to the best results of a century ago.* For example, the Report of the School Committee of Cambridge, Massachusetts for 1875, in a comparison of these results, says:

"*'There is reason to believe that more and better work was done by our schools in the early days of the Republic than is accomplished now.'*

"This report was written by Dr. A. P. PEABODY of Harvard College. Again, in an address delivered before the Massachusetts Convention of Teachers in January, 1876, Dr. PEABODY returns to the subject, thus:

"*'The schools of former generations in New England,* (in most other parts of the country the common school is a very modern institution,) though by any now recognized standard of comparison very far *in*ferior to the present, *did much more for their pupils than is done now.'*

" He says the former condition of things, its merits as well as demerits, has become obsolete; still he *'believes it accomplished more for the fit education of the citizens than is effected under the present regime.'* This testimony, given under the shadow of our oldest college, may be mistaken, but it cannot be whistled out of the way."

Omitting some repetitions, I believe that this is the sum of the testimony submitted by Mr. HINSDALE outside of the West Point argument and authorities. The latter are reserved for special consideration further on.

If this is all that requires attention just here, the query may be raised, why I reply at so great length as I shall do. In answer, let me say again, as I said at the beginning, that I shall not confine myself to the review of Mr. HINSDALE'S paper. He expresses here some very common prejudices in regard to the elementary instruction in our schools. The parties complaining have, as he says, " a right to be heard," and more than that, I would say that they have a right to ask of us to show the grounds on which we base our claims to improvement in the public

---

schools. Furthermore, I desire to collect and arrange, in convenient form, materials for others to use in the discussion of a question which is of immediate interest to all. Let us then hear the

COUNTER TESTIMONY.

It may be well enough to continue the evidence from Harvard College while we have the testimony of Dr. PEABODY fresh in mind. Let us then call the President of Harvard.

President ELIOT, in his inaugural address in 1869, said:

" The improvement of the schools has of late years permitted the College to advance the grade of its teaching, and adapt the methods of its later years to men instead of boys. This improvement of the College reacts upon the schools to their advantage, and this action and reaction will be continuous." *

Mr. ELIOT pronounced these words on the occasion of his inauguration, and in the presence of an assembly such as is rarely gathered together. The recollections of some there could verify or disprove what he said. The policy of the institution was shaped accordingly, the conditions of admission were greatly advanced, and yet Prof. PEABODY tells us in various phraseology, but always to the same effect: " There is reason to believe that more and better work was done by our schools in the early days of the Republic than is accomplished now." But let us next call one who some years ago occupied the chair which President ELIOT so worthily fills at the present time.

EDWARD EVERETT—a graduate in 1811, a Professor of Greek Literature and finally President of Harvard College, a Minister to England, a Governor of the State, and first Chairman of the Board of Education of the Commonwealth of Massachusetts—was certainly a man of high culture, and surely had "exceptional opportunities for observation." Of the preparatory schools,—Phillips'

---

* When this was read, President HINSDALE asked whether Mr. ELIOT speaks of the public schools. My reply was that I supposed he did not have them in mind at the time, but they could not be excluded for the reason that the public high schools are represented by many of the best members of the College. As I write this, I learn that the second in the sophomore class of some two hundred is a graduate of the West High School of this city, which is now represented there by six of its former pupils. The Boston boys, from the Public Latin School, on entering Harvard, usually take the head of the class. It is sometimes paradoxically said they are "too well prepared;" that is, they are so well fitted for the course that the first year's work does not sufficiently tax their powers.

4

Academy at Exeter, and the Boston Latin School, which I suppose had few if any equals in the country, he says:

"As to the learned languages and classical literature generally, they were
very poorly taught in those days. I do not like to speak disparagingly of
men and things gone by. The defects were at least *vitia aevi non hominum*,
but defects they were of the grossest kind. The study of the Latin and Greek
was confined to the cursory reading of the easier authors: a little construing
and parsing, as we called it. The idiom and genius of the languages were
not unfolded to us, nor the manner of the different writers, nor the various
illustrative learning necessary to render the text-book which was read intelli-
gible. We got the lesson to recite, and that was all." *

In one of his addresses, after an interesting description of the
discomforts and hardships of the boys in attendance upon the
Latin school of Boston during the earlier part of the present
century, Mr. Everett says:

" The standard of scholastic attainment was certainly not higher than that
of material comfort in those days. We read pretty much the same books, or
books of the same class in Latin and Greek as we read now, with the exception of the Greek Testament, but we read them in a very superficial manner.
'There was no attention paid to the philosophy of the languages, to the deduction of words from their radical elements, to the niceties of construction,
still less to prosody." †

And again :

"In fact, Mr. Chairman, there are few things in which the rapid progress of our country is so apparent as in the institutions for education. The
learned Secretary of the Board of Education (Rev. Dr. SEARS) has just
alluded to the defects of the schools in the most remote parts of the Commonwealth, unfavorably situated in this respect. I dare say his representations
are correct; but the younger part of this audience would not believe me, no
one scarcely whose own recollection did not confirm it, would believe me, if I
were to describe the state of what were called good schools when I was myself
a school-boy. * * * I allude to the condition of the best public schools of that
day." ‡

Hon. HENRY BARNARD, of Rhode Island, who has, perhaps,
made more valuable contributions to the history and literature of
American education than all others together, gives his testimony
as follows:

" It may be said with perfect truth that the schools and colleges were left
very much to haphazard. A person who could do nothing else was considered a
proper person to keep school; and though the College at Cambridge, where the
standard was at the highest, required of its few instructors some qualifications

---

* Barnard's American Journal of Education, Vol. VII., page 349.
† Barnard's American Journal of Education, Vol. VII., page 348.
‡ Barnard's American Journal of Education, Vol. VII., page 344.

higher than this of inability to serve the public elsewhere, its standard was as low as we have seen. There was no science of education in the country; there seems to have been little thought, much less hope of improving it. The schools and colleges were probably at not quite so high a standard as they were at some period before the Revolutionary War. Certainly they were no better."

The testimony of two such eminent witnesses, both "highly-cultured" men, and both of "exceptional opportunities for observation," is probably enough to show how much more the preparatory schools of former generations, in New England, did for their pupils than is now done!

Let us now turn to the common schools, and see how much " more and better work " they did than is accomplished now.

THE BOSTON COMMON SCHOOLS.

That the reader may understand the evidence pertaining to the schools of Boston, it will be best perhaps to explain their organization at the time of the Revolution and for fifty years thereafter. We shall do this, as far as possible, in the language of Mr. W. B. FOWLE, who probably entered the schools as a pupil about the year 1800, and who became in time a noted teacher and an author of many school books. Aside from the evidence, at which it is our main purpose to get, this sketch will not be without interest to any one who is engaged in the work of teaching, or who is interested in school affairs. It may be of service, too, as showing that the testimony adduced really covers the whole ground. Besides two Latin schools, in which only Latin and Greek were taught,* there were two other schools called

Writing Schools.—These were the only public schools of Boston up to 1790. Writing and arithmetic were the principal

---

* Boys had been admitted into the Latin schools at the early age of seven years; in 1790 the age was increased to ten years by the new system, but as before no provision was made in the Latin school for their instruction in English, in penmanship or in any of the common branches. "To remedy this serious defect, the Latin scholars were *allowed* to attend the writing schools two hours, forenoon and afternoon, and about thirty availed themselves of the privileges, although they were obliged to neglect one school to attend the other, and unpunctuality and disorder in all the schools were the natural consequences." But the teachers of the Latin schools also sometimes opened private schools, in which case the necessity of attending the writing schools was obviated. "The teachers of the Latin school in connection with a writing master, kept a private English school in the Latin school room, while the writer was a pupil there, in 1808, and the writer himself attended a private school kept by a *reading* master in another part of the town. Of course, it was a passport to favor in every public school to attend the master's private school also; and those who went only to the public school were considered a somewhat inferior caste." (W. B. Fowle, page 330, Vol. X, Barnard's American Journal of Education.)

branches taught. "Although reading and spelling were also taught
in them, this instruction was only incidental, being carried on—
we cannot say "attended to"—while the teachers were making or
mending pens preparatory to the regular writing lessons."

" 'The only schools in the city to which girls were admitted were kept by
the teachers of the public schools, between the forenoon and afternoon ses-
sions; and how insufficient this chance for an education was, may be gathered
from the fact that all the public teachers who opened (these) private schools
(for girls) were *uneducated men*, selected (for the writing schools) for their skill
in penmanship and in the elements of arithmetic." *

Reading Schools.—In 1790, girls were admitted for the first time
to the public schools of Boston. In consequence of the increased
number of pupils, and on account of the incompetency of the
writing masters, one more Writing School was established, and three
new schools, called " Reading Schools." One Writing and one
Reading School, were placed in a school building, one occupying
the first floor, the other the second. The boys and girls were
kept separate, the former attending one school in the morning
and the other in the afternoon, and the latter alternating with
them. The masters on the two floors were entirely independent
of each other. This " double-headed" system, as it was called,
was maintained down to about 1850, possibly in some schools
even later.

The studies pursued in these schools may be learned from two
extracts from the records : " One regulation requires the Writing
Masters to teach "writing and the branches (of arithmetic) *usually
taught in town schools*, including vulgar and decimal fractions."
"Another regulation required the Reading Masters to teach spelling, accent and the reading of prose and verse, and to instruct
the children in English Grammar, epistolary writing and composition." †

With this explanation, we may readily understand the following
passages taken from the Memoir of Mr. BINGHAM. In the light
of evidence like this, we may estimate the declaration of Mr.
PEABODY at its true value when he says that "there is reason to
believe that more and better work was done by our schools in the

* W. B. Fowle, in his Memoir of Caleb Bingham, Barnard's Journal, Vol. V, page 330.
† "Memoir of Caleb Bingham," Barnard's Journal, Vol. V, page 333.

early days of the Republic than is done now ;" and we shall duly appreciate the courage of Mr. HINSDALE when he avows the belief that the present results of the schools, and especially of the graded schools, "are inferior to the best results of a century ago."

THE WRITING SCHOOLS.

"Furthermore, it was ordered that in the writing schools the children should begin to learn arithmetic at eleven years of age; that at twelve they should be taught to make pens. Until eleven years old, all the pupils did in a whole forenoon or afternoon was to write one page of a copy-book not exceeding ten lines. When they began to cipher, it rarely happened that they performed more than two sums in the simplest rules. These were set in the pupil's manuscript, and the operation was there recorded by him. No printed book was used. Such writing and ciphering, however, were too much for one day, and the boys who ciphered only did so every other day.

"If it be asked, 'how were the three hours of school-time occupied ?' the answer is, in one of three ways: in mischief, in play or in idleness. The pupils were never taught to make their own pens, and it occupied the master and usher two hours of every session to prepare them. The books were generally prepared by them out of school hours. The introduction of metallic pens relieved the teachers from their worst drudgery, and left them free to inspect the writing of their pupils, which was impossible before."

THE READING SCHOOLS.

"In the reading schools, the course was for every child to read one verse of the Bible, or a short paragraph of the Third Part. The master heard the first and second, that is, the two highest classes, and the usher heard the two lowest. While one class was reading, the other studied the spelling lesson. The lesson was spelled by the scholars in turn, so that the classes being large, each boy seldom spelled more than one or two words.

"In grammar, the custom was to recite six or more lines once a fortnight, and to go through the book three times before any application of it was made to what was called parsing."

These statements will become to the reader living realities as he reads the following sketch of Mr. TILESTON, who is often kindly alluded to in Mr. EVERETT's school-addresses as one of the best teachers of his day. Mr. FOWLE says of him:

"He loved routine, and probably if he had taught school a century, he would never have improved any arrangement of it. Printed arithmetics were not used in the Boston schools until after the writer left them; and the custom was for the master to *write a problem or two in the manuscript of the pupil*

EVERY OTHER DAY. No boy was allowed to cipher till he was eleven years old, and writing and ciphering WERE NEVER performed on the same day. Master TILESTON had thus been taught by Master PROCTOR, and the sums he set for his pupils were copied exactly from his old manuscript. Any boy could copy the work from the manuscript of any further advanced than himself, and the writer never heard of any explanation of any principle of arithmetic while he was at school. Indeed, the pupil believed that the master could not do the sums he set for them; and a story is told of the good old gentleman, which may not be true, but which is so characteristic as to afford a very just idea of the course of instruction, as well as of the simplicity of the superannuated pedagogue. It is said that a boy who had done the sum set for him by Master TILESTON, carried it up, as usual, for examination. The old gentle-man, as usual, took out his manuscript, compared the slate with it, and pronounced it wrong. The boy went to his seat and reviewed his work, but finding no error in it, returned to the desk and asked Mr. TILESTON to be good enough to examine the work, for he could find no error in it. This was too much to require of him. He growled, as his habit was when displeased, but he compared the sum again, and at last with a triumphant smile exclaimed: 'See here, you *nurly* (gnarly) wretch, you have got it 'If four tons of hay cost so much, what will seven tons cost?' when it should●e, 'If four tons of *Eng- lish* hay cost so a so.' Now go and do it all over again.'"

The following "Memorandum of an eminent Clergyman, who was educated in the best schools in Boston just before the Revo- lation," we copy from a volume of the Massachusetts Common School Journal, Vol. XII, pages 311 and 312. The notes are by the editor of the Journal:

"At the age of six and a half years, I was sent to Master JOHN LOVELL'S Latin school. The only requirement was reading well; but, though fully quali- fied, I was sent away to Master GRIFFITH, a private teacher, to learn to read, write and spell." * * * "I learned the English Grammar in Dilworth's Spell- ing Book by heart. Entered LOVELL'S school at seven years. LOVELL was · a tyrant, and his system one of terror. Trouncing* was common in the school. * * * SAM. BRADFORD, afterward Sheriff, pronounced the P in Ptolemy, and the younger LOVELL rapped him over the head with a heavy ferule.† * * *

---

* Trouncing was performed by stripping the boy, mounting him upon another's back, and whipping him with birch rods before the whole school.

† We saw this done by another Boston teacher about thirty years ago, and when we remonstrated with him upon the danger of inflicting such a blow upon such a spot, 'O, the caitiffs,' said he, 'it is good for them !' About the same time another teacher, who used to strike his pupils upon the hand so that the marks and bruises were visible, was waited upon by a committee of mothers who lived near the school, and had been annoyed by the outcries of the sufferers. The teacher promised not to strike the boys any more upon the *hand*, and the women went away satisfied. But instead of inflicting blows upon the hand, he inflicted them upon the soles of the feet, and made the punishment more severe.

We studied Latin from 8 o'clock till 12, and from 1 till dark. * * * After one or two years, I went to the town school to Master HOLBROOK, at the corner of West street, to learn to write; and to Master PROCTOR, on Pemberton's Hill, in the southeast part of Schollay's Building. My *second, third* and *fourth years I wrote there, and did nothing else.*

"I entered college at the age of fourteen years and three months, and was, equal in Latin and Greek to the best in the *Senior Class.* Xenophon and Sallust were the only books used in college that I had not studied." * * *

"The last two years of my school life nobody taught English grammar or geography but Col. JOSEPH WARD, who was self-taught and set up a school in Boston. * * *

"*I never saw a map except in Cæsar's Commentaries, and did not know what that meant.* Our class studied Lowth's English Grammar at college. At Master PROCTOR's school, reading and writing were taught in the same room to girls and boys from seven to fourteen years of age, and the Bible was the only reading book. Dilworth's Spelling Book was used and the New England Primer. The master set sums in our MSS., but, did not go further than the Rule of Three."

The above testimony shows the amount and kind of work which was done in the Boston schools about the time of the Revolution, and from that period down to the end of the first decade of the present century. Many more pages might be filled with evidence to like effect ; but so long as this remains unquestioned, I refrain from adducing any more in regard to the education of youth in the earlier days of the Republic. But before we pass to a later period, I would respectfully ask whether it is possible for any man, in the exercise of ordinary good sense, to conceive the notion that schools such as have been brought before us in this testimony, "did more for their pupils than is now done," especially in the graded schools of our large towns and cities.

Let us now look at the work of the third and fourth decades. This period differs from the former in that it was marked by the beginning of a revival the results of which are just now making themselves felt. If, however, any one supposes that some magic power intervened to lift the schools to a higher plane, without the application of those agencies which we now rely upon to improve our systems of instruction, he will be soon convinced of his error if he will but glance over the pages of the "American Journal of Education," published in Boston from 1826 to 1830, and the "Annals of Education," which succeeded it from 1831 to

1839. WILLIAM RUSSELL, the editor of the former, and W. C. WOODBRIDGE, the editor of the latter, cannot yet be forgotten by American scholars. It is needless to say that anything which appeared under the names of these men, or which they endorsed is worthy of confidence. I have not space to quote from these volumes at any considerable length, and must therefore content myself with a few sentences which seem to summarize the opinions of only two or three of the most prominent contributors.

We first quote from an address on the "Common Errors of Education," which was delivered at Brooklyn, Conn., and which we find in Vol. IV of the "Journal." The author was Rev. SAMUEL J. MAY, who was one of the ablest men of his day, and was thoroughly acquainted with the quality of the education which prevailed at that time. Speaking of the little children who "are ranged on uncomfortable benches, condemned to sit still if possible, perhaps their hands folded, the greater part of three long hours in each half day, *literally doing nothing*," he says: "No attempt is made to excite thought, communicate ideas, to awaken curiosity, to impart knowledge." * * * "For months or a whole year they are kept drilling upon the alphabet, and for another year must pour over columns of syllables and words of which not one in twenty can they understand."

How different is the picture of the little children in the modern graded school, where, instead of that enforced idleness which stupifies, we find cheerful industry in that which educates while it interests the mind. How different the results. Instead of spending months or a year on the alphabet, and quite commonly a second year over the columns of a spelling book, the average child is now brought to the reading of one of the standard Second Readers in a single year ; in the same time he learns the combinations of integers in addition, subtraction, multiplication and division within the limit of tens ; he learns generally to write upon the slate whatever he can read, besides being taught music and drawing according to his capacity to learn. Surely this is progress, provided of course that the mind of the child be not over-taxed, of which there is little danger so long as his instruction partakes of the nature of amusement.

What Mr. MAY has to say about the teaching of grammar and geography is not to the point of the present inquiry, but he is equally severe in his comments on the prevailing errors of instruction in these branches; errors which left the intelligence about where they found it, and the higher faculties of the mind wholly untouched. Of arithmetic, he says in substance that it is taught in such a way that a child learns only the mechanical processes without so much as suspecting that there is a principle involved in the rules. In the common mode of teaching reading, he says that teachers allow children to "read, day after day and month after month, passages from which they receive no very definite ideas, until at last their pupils come to suppose that the whole art of reading consists in calling words correctly and rapidly in the succession in which they may happen to stand—this is, in fact, all that the greater part do acquire." Again, in speaking of reading the Bible, he says: " Thus the most momentous truths and sublime doctrines * * * are gabbled over merely as an exercise in what is called reading." *

Another writer,† whose name is not given, treats of the same subjects at greater length and quite as severely as Mr. MAY. By way of illustrating the almost universal defect in the methods of teaching arithmetic, he says of himself that he was "*never* made to comprehend" the rules of addition and subtraction, and became disheartened and embarrassed. He continues thus :

"True it is that I persevered, and after several years was able to 'cipher' with ease ; but my whole art was merely mechanical; I understood not the reason even of the simplest operation, and was able to resolve those problems only which were precisely similar to what I had formerly done. I never made any attempt at an ingenious analysis of complicated questions, but took the numbers and placed them in certain positions, added or subtracted, multiplied or divided agreeably to the direction of the rule, and when the answer appeared, could no more tell why it was the correct one than if it had been produced by the sleight of juggler, or had been the result of a chemical combination."

One would not risk much by saying that the experience of most of those who received their education thirty or forty years ago was

---

* American Journal of Education, 1829, Vol. IV., pp. 217—223.
† Vol. II, p. 157, American Journal of Education, Boston, 1827.

6

similar to that of the writer of the foregoing paragraph. Those
who have since become teachers bear almost unanimous testimony to this defect in their early instruction in this branch. Only
by subsequent study have they become aware how little they
understood of the subjects they had "ciphered" through in their
school days.

But let us turn to Vol. V. of the "Annals." Here we find,
among many other articles of interest and importance as bearing
on the subjects of our inquiry, notes of visits to the schools of
"one of the large commercial towns of the most enlightened part
of our country." The article is written at the request of the
editor, who remarks that the "names of persons and places are
omitted out of regard for the feelings of those concerned;" but
from some general remarks, and from the number of schools referred to, we judge that the place was the city of Boston. Of the
spelling exercises, he says that when one "guessed the right orthography" of a word, "he 'went up.'" Of the exercises in
arithmetic, he gives a description which would be ludicrous if it
were not of so serious a thing as the misspent time and energy
of thousands of children ; we can well afford to omit it after what
has been said by Mr. MAY and others on the same subject. In
regard to reading he says :

"I heard some of the pupils read from Pierpont's National Reader, and
from their manner of reading, I was almost led to conclude that they did not
learn anything." * * * "There was such a low mumbling of words that I
obtained but few ideas from what was passing over the lips of the reader; and
in the whole exercise there was evidently very little of mental activity."

In regard to writing, he says :

"A description of this exercise would be similar to that which should por-
tray the same exercise as exhibited in those country schools of New England
into which the spirit of improvement had not yet entered; where the teacher
sits in his chair and attends to his pupils as they are continually coming forward with 'bad pens.'"

On a preceding page I have represented the modes of government in the Boston schools; and inasmuch as this matter,
important as it will be conceded to be, is not in question, I will
not quote what the writer says about the loud, harsh tones
of the teachers, which saluted his ears in all the schools, nor of

the blows which he saw inflicted on the heads of the "little ones." Well may the writer raise the question : "If such is the state of the schools in one of the most highly-favored towns of the State, what can be expected from the smaller and less-favored villages and widely-extended townships ?" *

Passing to the ninth and last volume of the series, I find an extract from the Second Annual Report of HORACE MANN, the Secretary of the State Board of Education. He writes as follows in regard to the subject of "Reading and Reading Books :"

"My information is derived principally from the written statements of the School Committees of the respective towns—gentlemen who are certainly exempt from all temptation to disparage the schools they superintend. The result is, that more than eleven-twelfths of all the children in the reading classes in our schools do not understand the meaning of the words they read; that they do not master the sense of the reading lessons, and that the ideas and feelings intended by the author to be conveyed to, and excited in the reader's mind still rest in the author's intention." * * * "It would hardly seem that the combined efforts of all persons engaged could have accomplished more in defeating the true objects of reading."

Having submitted the testimony of men of high position and character, men as well or better known to the whole country for scholarship and general ability than Dr. PEABODY or Prof. CHURCH, men whose special business it was to examine into the work done in the schools from forty to a hundred years ago, and who may be supposed to have had an extensive knowledge of that of which they have affirmed; and finally of men who are known to have made a critical study of the methods of instruction appropriate to primary and grammar schools, having submitted the abundant and explicit testimony of such men, what can we think of the declaration of Prof CHURCH to the effect that we have made no improvement on the "good old system?" If we have not, it is in vain that PESTALOZZI, FROEBEL, MANN, BARNARD, HALL, CARTER, MAY, PEIRCE, PAGE, WOODBRIDGE, RUSSELL and EMERSON have lived and labored in this cause ; in vain have we in the present day studied the writings of these men, and tried to carry out the principles of education which they advocated ; and to sum up the whole matter, in vain is an attempt made to exercise reason in the management of educational affairs.

* Pp. 494—498, Vol. V., Annals of Education, 1835.

I raise no question as to the honesty or candor of the men who
have volunteered to give impulse to the reactionary feeling against
common schools, which is generally making itself felt throughout the country. That they think they are right is as unquestion-
able as the proof that they are wrong. They have manifestly
judged from insufficient data. Because they happened to fall
under the instruction of good teachers, they suppose that the
education of the State and nation was in good hands when they
were boys. One other hypothesis, that is that they do not see
things as they did when they were young, may be less obnoxious
to their pride. They may choose as they please either alternative :
one or the other they will have to accept.

How great the danger of error, in making up our judgments in
reference to such matters, is thus pointed out by HERBERT
SPENCER, in the " Study of Sociology," p. 79 :

"How testimonies respecting objective facts are thus perverted by the sub-
jective states of the witnesses, and how we have to be ever on our guard
against this cause of vitiation in sociological evidence may indeed be inferred from the illusions that daily mislead men in their comparisons of past
with present. Returning after many years to the place of his boyhood, and
finding how insignificant are the buildings he remembered as so imposing,
every one discovers that in this case it was not the past was so grand, but that
his impressibility was so great and his power of criticism so small. He does
not perceive, however, that the like holds generally ; and that the apparent
decline in various things, is really due to the widening of his experiences and
the growth of a judgment no longer so easily satisfied. Hence the mass of
witnesses may be under the impression that there is going on a change just the
reverse of that which is really going on ; as we see, for example, in the notion
current in every age, that the size and strength of the race have been de-
creasing, when, as proved by bones, by mummies, by armour, and by the
experiences of travellers in contact with aboriginal races, they have been on
the average increasing."

Turning from this more general evidence into which I have
been led, I submit the following extract from the Report of the
Superintendent of the Schools of Boston, for the year 1857. It
will serve to show how slow the march of progress has been where
circumstances have been most favorable. Mr. PHILBRICK says :

"In my visits, it was very uncommon to hear in any of these schools a
single question or remark by the teacher which had any reference to the understanding of the children. In many cases, the reading was but little more than

the mechanical pronunciation of an unknown tongue. There is a text-book in daily use in all these schools entitled 'Spelling and Thinking Combined;' but in all the exercises in this book, I never saw the slightest evidence of any attempt at the combination indicated in the title.

"Another general defect is *the want of profitable employment for the children* especially in the lowest classes. Go into any of these schools any time of day, and in nine cases out of ten, if not forty-nine out of fifty, three-fourths of the pupils will be found without *profitable* employment. Thus the time of these children is wasted for precious months and years in succession. But this great waste of time is not the only evil arising from this defect. Many bad habits are formed. The strength of the teacher, which should be expended in teaching, is necessarily taxed to a great extent by the incessant vigilance and care requisite to keep these idlers out of mischief, and to secure some reasonable degree of stillness."

THE DISTRICT SCHOOL AND OTHER MEANS OF EDUCATION.

If the Boston schools, which enjoyed every advantage of the times, were in the condition indicated in the foregoing testimony, what shall we infer in regard to the schools of the smaller towns and in the rural districts, which were in session only a few weeks each year. There is no lack of evidence to show that the natural inference is the correct one, namely, that they were sadly deficient in every important particular. Speaking of the condition of the schools as they were at the close of the Revolution, SALEM TOWN, whose opportunities for observation were unequaled, and whose reliability is beyond question, says:

" The time during which the schools were taught in the rural districts—and such were most of them at the close of the Revolution—was from *eight* to *twelve weeks*, and that in the winter season. In the summer there were few if any schools, as all who could hoe a hill of corn or do housework were required to labor. At this early period the attainments of those who had no further instruction than was received in the district school were limited to very few branches, the reasons for which are quite obvious, namely: the *inability of the teachers* on the one part, and the limited time of attendance allowed by the parents on the other. Spelling, Reading, Writing, and Arithmetic as far as the Rule of Three with Simple Interest, were the main branches. It was however thought by many parents unnecessary to have their daughters taught in arithmetic, as in their view it would be of little or no use to them. Fractions were out of the question." *

To cipher through the Rule of Three, exclusive of Fractions, at fourteen years of age, was considered quite an achievement.

° Barnard's Journal of Education, Vol. XIII., p. 739.

As limited as was the course in arithmetic, we are told by Mr. BURTON that it was taught without so much as an attempt at the explanation of rules and principles. The "carrying of tens" in addition, and "borrowing" in subtraction, were " unaccountable operations." *

The Rev. HEMAN HUMPHREY, for twenty years President of Amherst College, and for many years a teacher in the schools of Connecticut, his native State, writing of the schools as they were about the year 1800, says :

" The branches taught were reading, spelling and writing, besides the A B C's to children scarcely four years old. * * * Our school books were the Bible, Spelling Book, and Webster's Third Part mainly. One or two others were found in some schools for the reading classes. Grammar was hardly taught at all in any of them, and that little was confined to committing and reciting the rules. Parsing was one of the occult sciences in my day. We had some few lessons in geography by questions and answers, bnt no maps, no globes; and as for black-boards, such a thing was never thought of till long years after. Children's reading and picture books we had none. * * * Arithmetic was hardly taught at all in the day-schools. As a substitute, there were some evening schools in most of the districts. * * * The winter schools were commonly kept about three months, in some favored districts four, but rarely so long. As none of what are now called the higher branches were taught beyond the merest elements, parents generally thought that three or four months were enough. * * * With regard to the summer schools of that period I have very little to say. They were taught by females upon very low wages, about as much a week as they could earn in families by spinning or weaving. * * * As we had no grammar schools in which the languages were taught, we most of us fitted for college with our ministers, who, though not very fresh from their classics, did what they could to help us." †

In many schools it was the custom to read four times a day, and each child expected to read each time. In reference to this matter, a prominent authority on this subject says :

" Had they read but once or twice, and but little at a time, and that with nice and very profitable attention to tone and sense, parents would have thought the master most miserably deficient in his duty, and their children cheated out of their rights, notwithstanding the time thus saved should be most assiduously devoted to other important branches of education.

" It ought not to be omitted that the Bible, particularly the New Testament, was the reading twice a day generally for all the classes adequate to words of

---

* The District School as it Was, by "One who went to it," (Rev. WARREN BURTON,) Boston, 1833, p. 114.

† Barnard's American Journal of Education, Vol. XIII., pp. 127, 128.

more than one syllable. It was the only reading of several of the younger classes under some teachers. On this practice I shall make but a single remark: as far as my own experience and observation extend, reverence for the sacred volume was not deepened by this constant and exceedingly careless use." *

The same writer says the principal requirement in reading was to "speak up loud and mind the stops." "As for suiting the tone to the meaning, no such thing was dreamed of, in our school at least. As much emphasis was laid on an insignificant *of* or *and*, as on the most important word in the piece." In regard to spelling, we are informed that though the pupils were found to be able to spell all the "monstrous great words" of the long spelling columns, they could not "spell the names of the most familiar things."† This is the kind of spelling that was taught in the schools of that day,—the spelling of which we hear so many boasts.

SAMUEL G. GOODRICH, in his "Recollections of a Lifetime," gives even more positive evidence to the same effect in regard to every point here touched upon.

Notwithstanding many faults incident to the times, there were some good schools in the past. The Phillips Academy was such, and perhaps a few others ; but that the common schools were far below the schools of the present, is clearly implied in many ways. The pupil who made the utmost out of the opportunities afforded in the meager course of study provided, received an education which was little short of a burlesque compared with what may be received at present in almost any city or town of the North. The superiority of the schools of the present is clearly implied in the expression so often met with in biographical sketches, that "the early education which he received was such as the times afforded."

Go into any public library, as I have done into the library of this city. Take down one biography after another and, unless the subject happens to be of exceptionally cultured parentage or large wealth, if his education be spoken of at all, you will, four times out of five, find a record such as would put to blush those who assure us that the schools of the past were superior to those of

---

* District School as it Was, Boston, 1833, pp. 52 to 55.

† District School as it Was, p. 146.

to-day; that is, if they know anything of the schools of the present, as in most cases we suspect they do not. Some of these will show that the college did the work in some departments now required in our lower grammar and even primary grades. In Tyler's Life of ROGER B. TANEY (born 1777), we find a sketch from which we may infer the condition of the schools in all that section of the country from which Dickinson College gathered its patronage. It is stated that all students in the college were required to purchase a small " Rhyming Geography," which had been written by the vice Principal and Lecturer on History, Natural Philosophy and Geography, and that the contents of the little book had to be committed to memory. The book contained about fifty pages, printed in octavo, and was an enumeration of the countries and nations of the world, and the principal rivers, mountains and cities in each of them.

* * * " It filled our minds with names of places and descriptions, without giving us any definite idea of their position on the globe or their relation to one another; and as may be supposed, some of the lines and rhymes were harsh and uncouth enough to be the subject of ridicule."

I cannot refrain from asking how the above work in geography, required by a Vice President of Dickinson College, compares with the " one-bean-and-two-beans-make-three-beans " exercise in our schools for the very youngest children just beginning to read, to which Dr. PEABODY refers in the passage quoted by Mr. HINS-DALE. But the above work in Geography was a part of Mr. TANEY'S *college course.* It is now—excepting the rhyme—the work of our primary schools.

In the memoirs of Dr. ELIPHALET NOTT, for sixty years the President of Union College, we find the following, in reference to the schools as they were in his youth and early manhood. He was born in 1773. The schools of Connecticut, his native State, are here spoken of:

" The country school of that day, in many districts at least, was a most unpromising institution. The teacher was not unfrequently a person of barely education enough to satisfy the critical requirements of some illiterate committee-man to whom was delegated the office of Examiner. He had perhaps left the shoe-bench, the anvil or the plow to try his hand for a few weeks at this easier work—to return at the close of his brief engagement to his more fitting business. The emolument could hardly have tempted him to turn teacher, for the pay was only from three to five dollars a month, and two months during the winter season was the usual term that the schools remained open. The teacher's office, therefore was not at that time a very inviting one, nor did the school he presided over hold out any strong inducements to parents who desired most of all to have their children well taught."

LYMAN BEECHER, in his Autobiograpy, says of his early education :

"I went in arithmetic through the Rule of Three, but nobody ever explained anything—we only did sums."

After his sixteenth year, Mr. BEECHER came under the instruction of Parson BRAY, who fitted boys for college. Of the instruction which he received in arithmetic, he says : "He gave us sums to do in arithmetic, but never explained. I suffered in that department from his neglect." And again : "In my sophomore year I did comparatively little. My early instructors had never explained the principles of arithmetic so that for this part of the course I had small qualification. Mathematics I lost totally."

The lives of Judge TANEY and Drs. NOTT and BEECHER were all that I could consult in the hour or two which I had snatched from more important duties. I found no testimony to conflict with that of the eminent men whom I have named.

We have quoted incontrovertible evidence to the effect that the common schools of New England, with few exceptions, were open from *two to four months* only in the year, and yet Dr. PEABODY is quoted as saying that their vacations were hardly a week in the year, (HINSDALE, p. 19.) The "all-system" schools, or graded schools, to call them by their proper name, now continue from nine to ten months in the year, and yet Dr. PEABODY says "the amount of time and energy devoted to it by those under instruction is *very much less* than it used to be." Does Dr. PEABODY know what the schools of the day are ? Does he know that the classification, which he views with so much horror, is simply a "plan" by which children are grouped in classes each "according to his or her proficiency," which he so greatly admires in the schools of the past ? He says "more and better work was done then than now." How *more* in one-third the time, and with attention given only to reading, writing, spelling, and arithmetic to the Rule of Three, fractions being beyond the question ? How *better*, when, as we have seen by competent testimony, the principles of arithmetic, were, so far as we can learn, never taught ; when two or three years were devoted to the definitions and rules of grammar without application to either analysis or composition ; when geography received comparatively little or no attention? Where in all New England were the common schools in any large numbers in session during the entire year, with only a few weeks' vacation? Private schools or small classes may have been thus taught by some retired clergyman who fitted boys for college.   There may have been some larger schools in the Dummer or Phillips Academies which had a continuous session through the year, but they were remarkable as exceptions to the rule.

We have thus far glanced at the history of common schools in the two leading States of New England down to 1836. We have seen *how* the " cuttings from the New England tree were planted, and how they grew in the Middle Atlantic and in the older and more prosperous of the Western States.

We have also submitted the testimony of school examiners and other school officers, of legislators and men of exceptional culture and opportunity for observation, to show what the condition of popular education was from 1836 to about the time of the breaking out of the civil war, a time which lies within the memory of the youngest members of this association.

And finally, we have had an interior view of the school-rooms, and we have seen the schoolmaster of one, two or three generations ago at work, and we have seen how he and his pupils did so " much more and better work than is now done ;" and this testimony we have had from the very men who suffered the disadvantages of those days.

The information we have gathered shows conclusively :

1. That Mr. Hinsdale's studies of the history and progress of the common school system are entirely at fault, and that his " rapid sketch " is the creation of fancy rather than fact.

2. That the present free public school system of the country is almost the creation of men, some of whom are still living and active in the work which they began in the full maturity of their powers.

3. That, as a consequence, the system cannot be saddled with the responsibility which might justly be laid upon an institution founded more than two centuries ago, and fostered by the liberality of generations.

4. That it is only here and there that the more enterprising
centers of wealth and intelligence have received the advantages of
the regenerated public-school system, just as the highest mountain
peaks are first gilded by the light of the morning sun.

5. That the surprising increase of expenditures which President HINSDALE parades on page nine is a practical result of
the almost fatal lesson which was taught us by the civil war, that
the common school is the only guarantee of political or personal
freedom.

This review of the history of our common school education
till within so late a period, will serve also to show how utterly
baseless are the deductions which are made by Mr. HINSDALE
from the West Point examinations, for when the products of the
schools, at their lowest point of degradation, were offering themselves for admission to West Point, the results of examinations
seem to have beeh best.   But we propose a different treatment of
the

WEST POINT ARGUMENT.

After casting about for a standard of measurement whereby the
results of the education to-day may be compared with that of
former generations, especially of forty or fifty years ago, President
HINSDALE remarks :

"Perhaps the best standard that occurs is the West Point examinations,
particularly the examinations of candidates for admission to the Academy.
Here is a large number of candidates each year; they come from all parts
of the Union; they are of about the same age, they are examined by
experienced teachers, generally holding their places during good behavior.
Fortunately a record of these examinations has been kept for nearly forty
years.   The results have been tabulated and published.   All educators and
especially common school teachers should be interested in the verdict that
West Point has given of our *common schools.*"

Reference is then made to the Report of the Board of Visitors
of 1875, in which the very suggestive fact is pointed out "that in
the last five years the average number of rejected candidates has
been six per cent. for physical disability, and forty per cent. for
deficiency in the scholastic requirements."   Then a point is made
that " in the six New England States, where educational facilities
are open to all, the rejections bave been thirty-five per cent. of the
number examined from that section."   Then comes the deduction: "*From these statistics, it is clearly evident that in the schools of
the country there is need of more thorough methods of instruction in
the elementary branches.*" This is from the Board of Visitors, and

by way of endorsement, they insert a memorandum from Prof. CHURCH, which concludes with this sentence: "I think our candidates are not as thoroughly prepared as they were twenty years ago." President HINSDALE, with some triumph, asks:

"Now what have our public school teachers to say to this? What do they propose to do with an old West Point examiner who charges some 'serious defect in their methods of teaching the elementary branches, particularly arithmetic, reading and spelling?'" * * * "But the West Point authorities furnish the evidence on which they base their indictment of the public schools. Part of it is found in the following:"

STATEMENT.

Showing the Number of Candidates for Cadetships appointed to the United States Military Academy, the Number Rejected, and the Number Admitted,

FROM 1838 TO 1876, INCLUSIVE.

YEAR.	NO. APPOINTED.	REJECTED BY ACADEMIC BOARD.	For Want of Qualification in—							REJECTED BY MEDICAL BOARD.	ADMITTED.	Of whom there GRADUATED four years thereafter—
			Reading.	Writing.	Orthography.	Arithmetic.	Grammar.	Geography.	History.			
1838..	132	2	1	1	1	1	0	0	0	1	111	54, or 48.6 per cent.
1839..	91	2	0	0	1	2	0	0	0	1	76	34, or 44.7 per cent.
1840 .	106	8	0	1	1	8	0	0	0	2	84	22, or 26.1 per cent.
1841..	131	8	6	4	1	6	0	0	0	0	114	34, or 29.8 per cent.
1842..	144	17	4	5	6	8	0	0	0	0	109	47, or 43.1 per cent.
1843..	77	6	0	5	5	4	0	0	0	8	60	29, or 48.3 per cent.
1844..	96	14	4	7	1	13	0	0	0	1	75	34, or 45.3 per cent.
1845..	98	9	3	1	1	7	0	0	0	1	81	40, or 49.3 per cent.
1846..	121	5	2	0	2	4	0	0	0	1	103	41, or 39.8 per cent.
1847..	84	1	1	0	1	0	0	0	0	3	74	35, or 47.2 per cent.
1848..	84	2	1	1	2	2	0	0	0	0	81	38, or 46.9 per cent.
1849..	95	0	0	0	0	0	0	0	0	2	88	42, or 47.7 per cent.
1850..	98	3	1	2	2	2	0	0	0	2	90	40, or 44.4 per cent.
1851..	81	3	1	3	3	3	0	0	0	0	71	31, or 43.5 per cent.
1852..	102	7	4	5	5	4	0	0	0	3	90	44, or 48.8 per cent.
1853..	97	6	2	2	2	5	0	0	0	1	83	36, or 39.7 per cent.
1854..	120	4	0	2	2	2	0	0	0	4 {47 56}	103	{20, 4 yrs., or 42.5 p. ct. 22, 5 yrs., or 39.2 p. ct.}
1855..	99	7	4	6	6	2	0	0	0	7	80	37, 5 yrs., or 46.2 p. ct.
1856..	101	17	2	5	12	6	0	0	0	4	72	44, 5 yrs., or 61.1 p. ct.
1857..	132	26	8	19	18	13	0	0	0	9	82	32, or 39 per cent.
1858..	108	19	6	12	11	13	0	0	0	4	75	24, or 32 per cent.
1859..	91	26	8	24	24	8	0	0	0	0	60	20, or 33.3 per cent.
1860..	84	12	4	7	7	7	0	0	0	0	72	27, or 37.5 per cent.
1861..	148	13	3	4	4	10	0	0	0	2	107	63, or 58.8 per cent.
1862..	96	11	1	8	7	4	0	0	0	0	81	38, or 46.9 per cent.
1863..	126	9	4	6	6	6	0	0	0	1	99	58, or 58.5 per cent.
1864..	101	15	4	11	11	9	0	0	0	0	73	46, or 63 per cent.
1865..	101	16	8	13	12	12	0	0	0	4	74	36, or 48.6 per cent.
1866..	95	17	7	9	9	13	0	0	0	1	70	45, or 64.2 per cent.
1867..	84	19	2	15	10	8	8	7	9	1	55	33, or 60 per cent.
1868..	127	34	8	12	12	16	25	15	19	3	76	53, or 72.5 per cent.
1869..	112	24	5	13	13	9	17	13	13	7	70	40, or 59.1 per cent.
1870..	163	73	15	30	30	28	54	42	40	4	65	37, or 56.9 per cent.
1871..	131	32	3	10	10	15	24	15	22	11	76	43, or 56.57 per cent.
1872..	165	35	0	19	19	11	17	18	15	20	95	
1873..	230	74	5	28	28	30	50	49	29	13	118	
1874..	175	66	4	25	25	30	46	36	19	4	89	
1875..	206	68	4	31	31	24	35	27	30	6	121	
1876..	167	53	4	22	22	23	31	17	21	3	98	

It is asked, what answer we have to make to this indictment? I confess that I am at a loss what to say, or rather what to say first. Nevertheless, let us begin by inquiring who these examinees are.

First. We find that each Congressional and Territorial District and the District of Columbia is, at any one time, entitled to *one* cadet at the Military Academy, and no more. Appointments at large, not to exceed ten, are also made annually.

Second. The district appointments are made on nomination of the member of Congress representing the district at the date of the appointment. The appointments at large are made by the President of the United States.

Third. The law requires that the appointee shall be a resident of the district from which he is appointed; and

Fourth. That he shall be from seventeen to twenty-two years of age.

Having been appointed, and being qualified as to age and residence, he can go to West Point for examination. If he pass the Academic and Medical Boards, he is admitted; if he fail, his failure is entered against the public schools,* and he is sent home again.

The fact that he made the attempt may be known only to himself and the member who appointed him; his absence from home can be attributed to a visit to New York; the whole matter escapes public notice, and no one will be held responsible for the failure but—the public schools. His name may never have been entered upon the rolls of a public school; † or if it has, he may

---

* That is, by those who take only a superficial view of the matter.

† If from a southern State, the chances are ten to one against it. See preceding statements as to the condition of the public schools in the South. If from a northern State, the chances are about one out of five that he never attended the public schools for any great length of time. It is a very common thing to send boys who do not succeed in the public schools from one private school to another where the little chance they might have for an education is lost by frequent change. Every year we hear of some of the most worthless pupils of the public schools going to some so-called colleges where they are admitted to higher studies to gratify the ambition of foolish parents and to secure patronage without which the "college" would go down. It is more than probable that those who are referred to by President CHURCH as giving long lists of collegiate studies, the "names of which are often misspelled," come from this very class. Whose fault is it that they escaped the common school and were *admitted* to "college" before they had learned to spell at least tolerably or learned the "elements of arithmetic and grammar?"

have been withdrawn before he even commenced some, at least,
of the studies required for admission, or he may have been* so
irregular in attendance, or so idle and indifferent, or so wanting
in brains, as never to have made any real progress—it matters
not to our Professor at West Point—his failure is set down to
serious defects in our common-school instruction,* especially in
the elementary branches.

Now, is it possible that this vicious system of appointment has
escaped the notice of Prof. CHURCH, Gen. SHERMAN and President HINSDALE? Have they not learned that the results of such
a system of patronage have been uniformly the same in every
country in which anything like it has been attempted, and that its
defects have caused it to be abandoned in almost every other
country than our own?

If these gentlemen have not heard the voice of successive Boards
of Visitors, or of the First Superintendent of the Academy on this
subject, it is because they have willfully closed their ears against
it. Col. THAYER, Superintendent of the Academy from 1816 to
1831, to whom the Academy is greatly indebted for the efficiency
of its present organization, protested against it repeatedly during
his time of service and afterward. In the Report of the Board of
Visitors for 1863, allusion is boldly made to the favoritism which
procured appointments for those who were found to be physically
disqualified, as well as mentally incompetent.

But having seen how irresponsible those are who make the appointments, that the appointments may be made indifferently
from all classes of schools, and in fact without regard to previous
school attendance, etc., let us turn to the question,

HAVE THE ACADEMIC EXAMINATIONS BEEN UNIFORM?

Prof. CHURCH writes to Mr. HINSDALE as follows:

"I do not think we have raised our standard of requirement in any one
branch. As far as possible we have endeavored to keep this the same from
year to year, though we have lately been more strict in our preliminary

* We do not say that boys who were totally incompetent may not have gone up with the
endorsement of public school teachers. We claim no more for common school men than may
be claimed for instance by the judiciary, not a few of whom have stained the ermine by
taking so much money in hand for given decisions; nor more than can be claimed for clergymen, many of whom have disgraced their holy calling. But we do claim that exceptional
cases should not be set down as the general rule.

examinations, and thus perhaps discover more deficiences than we would under a less vigorous system."

What this may mean is not very clear. "The standard of requirement in no one branch has been raised, though we have lately been more strict in our examinations." "Preliminary," of course, for that's what we are talking of. What is greater strictness exercised for, but to "discover more deficiencies," to exact more thorough knowledge of principles, and greater accuracy in applying them? Why the uncertainty of the "perhaps," as if greater strictness was not certain to exclude candidates who would be admitted "under a less vigorous system?" How delicate of the marksman who would say: "I take my station nearer the target; my nerve is steadier, my aim is more accurate, and *perhaps* that is the reason I hit the bull's eye oftener than I used to do."

Prof. MICHIE states t he case more plainly when he says:

"Since 1870 the examinations have been written and the character of the examinations much more severe, although the scope is the same."

This we can comprehend, and those of us who know what written examinations mean, understand why it is that so many more fail than formerly. That the examinations are more severe, though the principal, is not the only reason. Another one quite as effective is, that the examinations *are in writing.* One-half of the candidates perhaps have never attempted to make up a manuscript on any subject till they come to West Point for examination. Few of us are aware how very little of such work is done in the "no-system" school of the country, even at the present time. The most of us witnessed the effect when written examinations were first introduced into graded schools.

As we have seen, Prof. CHURCH gives his testimony with a kind of delicate apprehensiveness, lest we should think the examinations had become too severe. Prof. MICHIE gives his as a statement of fact, without any concern as to its effect, but both make their statements with proper official caution. They speak of the institution with which their own reputation is closely associated. But members of the Board of Visitors speak with less reserve when they say, as I heard a very prominent educator* say not

---

* Hon. B. G. NORTHROP, Secretary of the State Board of Education, Connecticut, author of "Education Abroad," "Education in Japan," etc.

long ago, in a Convention of School Superintendents : "There is no comparison as to severity between their examinations to-day and those of twenty years ago." The graduates of the Academy, however, put it still more effectively when they characterized the examination of a few years ago at West Point as a farce, the broadness of which at any given time depended on how many students were wanted to fill up the institution. But if further evidence were wanting, there is abundant evidence of a variable standard in the table itself.

INTERNAL EVIDENCE OF A VARIABLE STANDARD.

In 1859 the number of rejections for poor writing and bad spelling was more than one in four of all examined ; two years thereafter, about one in thirty-five. In 1869, eight per cent. failed in arithmetic ; the very next year, sixteen per cent. In 1870, for deficiencies in grammar, over thirty-three per cent. were rejected ; two years after, ten per cent. In 1870, fifteen out of one hundred and sixty-three were rejected for poor reading ; in 1872, out of one hundred and sixty-five, none ! I have selected a few only of the more striking cases. The reader will find the table full of them. If the candidates of one year came from one section, and those of another year came from another section, we could interpret the result by some other theory than that the examinations are variable ; but as it is, there can be no other conclusion than that Mr. HINSDALE'S best standard has been very elastic.

But it may be objected that these are merely accidental variations. Take then periods of five years each:

From 1850 to 1855 the rejections were 5 per cent. of the examined.
" 1855 to 1860 " 25 " "
" 1860 to 1865 " 12 " "
" 1865 to 1870 " 24 " "
" 1870 to 1875 " 38 " "
" 1875 & 1876 " 36 " "

Who is there so credulous that he could be convinced by this or indeed any amount of testimony that the average scholarship of young men of the nation was so much better from 1850 to 1855 than it was the five years following ; or, if it had fallen away so greatly, who would believe that it improved one hundred per cent. in the next five years, only to decline again in a like period to its former condition?

If the examiners had constituted successive classes in any one institution under teachers changing every five years, this great difference would be something rather remarkable, but that the average scholastic attainments of a whole people could so change eclipses our conception of possibility.

See what remarkable pranks this wonderfully magic measure plays with the New England States. The Board of Visitors of 1875 direct attention to the fact that,

" In the six New England States, where educational facilities are open to all, the rejection has been 35 *per cent.* of the number examined from that section."

This statement comprises one paragraph; the next, which is equally brief, contains this deduction :

" From these statistics it is clearly evident that in the schools of the country there is need of more thorough methods of instruction in the elementary branches."

Before we refer to the table from which the Visitors derive these statements, we may remark that the latter paragraph would sound quite as well and seem far more reasonable if it read thus :

From these statistics, it is clearly evident that many young men are appointed who have not completed the course of an ordinary district school. Or, they might have put it thus : From these statistics, it is evident that many young men are sent up for examination from the so-called colleges and academies, who have not native ability or industry enough to master the studies of the common schools.

But let us take a few items from the table referred to (by the Visitors), and arrange them so that we can take in at a glance some startling comparisons between the last five and the preceding thirty-two years.

7

The number from the New England States examined and rejected from 1838 to 1874:

	THIRTY-TWO YEARS. 1838 to 1870.		FIVE YEARS. 1870 to 1874, incl.	
	EXAMINED.	REJECTED.	EXAMINED.	REJECTED.
Maine......................	55	1	13	5
New Hampshire............	31	2	5	1
Vermont...................	34	2	3	0
Massachusetts	94	0	23	7
Rhode Island..............	20	0	5	2
Connecticut	45	3	11	5
Total.................	279	8	60	20
	Less than 3 per cent.		33⅓ per cent.	

Now, what is the probability in this case? Is it that the New England States had floated on—an educated people educating their children—for thirty-three years losing less than three out of the hundred examined,* during even the last five years of that period feeling no apprehension of approaching disaster,†—only to plunge at once into such an abyss of ignorance? Or, is not rather more probable that the examinations of the last five years represented in the table, were much more severe than they had been before? What would you say, Mr. President, even though Prof. MICHIE and others had not said they were—taking for granted then what cannot be denied, viz: that the examinations are much more severe than they used to be, and knowing, as you must, that appointments are often made with reckless disregard of public interest—were you not able to account for the increased ratio of failures, without suspecting any great deterioration in the teaching of reading and writing, spelling and ciphering in the schools of New England?

But strange to say, we find a parallel to this wonderful shuttle-cock, a nation's scholarship, in the almost as wonderful variation

---

* A thing in itself to be wondered at unless the candidates had been chosen with extreme caution.

† Only two had been rejected from all New England from 1865 to 1870.

of the physical condition of its male youth. While statistics of health show that chronic ailments maintain a nearly constant average throughout the United States from year to year, the statistics of West Point seem to indicate the most astounding fluctuations.

From 1860 to 1870, out of 1,074 appointments, only 16 were rejected by the Medical Board ; within the last five years covered by the table, 52 were rejected out of 864.* Have physical infirmities among our young men really trebled within ten years? If they have, how long will it take for us to become a nation of chronic invalids? What will become of the boast of Americans, that they are physically superior to any other people of the globe? What becomes of medical statistics, showing that the physical condition of the civilized races is improving and the length of life increasing? But our alarm is changed to confidence when we turn to a later table, which is to be found in the " Register of the Military Academy for the year 1876." We there find that only one in fifty was rejected by the Medical Board from 1874 to 1876, to one in twelve the three preceding years.

Now, it is not necessary that we declare such opposite results, either of scholarship or soundness of "wind and limb," to be impossible. Though, as we have said, we believe them to be results of varying standards of measurement, carelessness of appointment may go far to explain them ; but it does not matter whether they are explained or not ; all that is necessary for us to know is, that they do not indicate the intellectual or physical status of the nation at one time as compared with another.

But there is one other way in which the table seems to discredit Prof. CHURCH's declaration that the standard of admission has not been raised as well as the other statement which he makes, that " while the proportion rejected has increased," he " finds as well in those admitted less accuracy in definitions and rules, less ability to give clear reasons, and less facility in the application of the principles whenever required in other branches of their mathematical course."

* Some confusion may arise from the fact that the tabular statement on page 52 includes the statistics of two years more than Mr. HINSDALE's table.

With such rapidly growing inferiority of the material how is it
that the ratio of graduations has increased more than fifty per
cent. within thirty or forty years? The following table certainly
needs explanation in the light of Professor CHURCH's declaration
which is quoted above.

*Table showing the number admitted, and the number and per cent. of
graduates for the time covered by the table given by President
Hinsdale, which is to be found on page 52.*

YEARS.	ADMITTED.	GRADUATED FOUR YEARS AFTERWARDS.	PER CENT.
38—43	494	191	37
43—48..........	393	179	46
48—53..........	420	195	46
53 58....	420	191	45
58—63..........	395	172	43*
63—68...	371	218	58
68—73	382	218	57

There is yet another light in which it will be interesting to con-
sider this table. It is assumed to be a "standard of measurement" whereby the value of the common education of one generation may be compared with that of another generation. If it be
accepted for this purpose, it surely may be taken as a fit standard
for the comparison of one State with another at the same time.
In applying it to the latter use that which we have discovered to
be the chief source of error is eliminated, viz: the variation of
the standard, for surely we may rely upon the Academic Board to
do even-handed justice to the several States at one and the same
sitting. Let us then compare the common education of some
of the States as ascertained by the West Point standard, with
the condition of education in the same States as ascertained by
the census of 1870.

It is supposed that this falling off may be accounted for by the withdrawal of some cadets
from the South at the breaking out of the Civil War.

The following table shows the comparative results of the two modes of ascertaining the quality of our common education :

STATES.	Number out of 1,000 White Males between 15 and 21, who cannot Write.	Per Cent. Rejected at West Point Examinations, since 1870.
Florida	325	0
Massachusetts	37	32
Ohio	53	34
New York	32	37
Virginia	246	37
Maine	31	40
Pennsylvania	40	42
Maryland	82	43
Connecticut	42	45

The above tabular statement needs no comment. The great educational metre discovered by Professor CHURCH, so far from being moved by varying degrees of public education is really not affected by extremes of either culture or ignorance. Its hands are moved over the dial face sometimes with wonderful rapidity, but they are not moved one way by the influence of good schools and contrariwise by the presence of illiterate youth. The power that moves them is amenable to no law. Each successive congressional representative turns the pointer this way or that as whim, caprice or motive, high or low chances to rule him as he passes along ; then the examiner calls "six," nine or three or anything else that he pleases, and the record which he makes is gravely urged to prove "the inferiority of our elementary instruction."

One last appeal to our judges, an *argumentum ad hominem*, and I shall leave them to decide the case as they please.

Take one of the five thousand youths of a congressional district who may be eligible to an appointment, take him pretty much at hap-hazard without regard to previous school attendance, industry or native capacity, would you judge the efficiency of the teachers of that district by the specimen? If you would, O ye professors and echoing visitors ! let us apply the measure to your school— the great standard of American military science. Let good men with a large number who are not so good, boon companions, creditors, debtors, political jobbers, bribe-takers or bribe-givers, every four years pick out those whom they may be pleased or whom it is their interest to call representatives of the Academy ; let these specimens of your work (?) be selected from among those whom you have discharged for incapacity from the first month to the beginning of the fourth year of the academic course ; let now and then one be taken at hap-hazard or by selection from among your graduates, and take some, perhaps a third, who have never entered the Military Academy, and let them all be placed in the hands of competent examiners to pass a technical examination on your entire course—the graduates, good, fair and indifferent, those whom you have "plucked" from stage to stage and even the strangers to your gate—with what justice could some congressional committee in reporting the result, make such complaint as the following :

From these results it is clearly evident that notwithstanding the large sums expended for its support, there is somewhere a serious defect in the system of instruction at West Point, especially in the simplest elements of a military course, Algebra, Geometry, etc.

What would you say to such a judgment ? Would you not say that it was a somewhat violent exhibition of insanity ? What then shall Massachusetts educators say to you ? Might they not say, "The country expects of men in the high position which you hold that they should '*think before they speak.*'"

SUMMARY OF THE REASONS WHY THE WEST POINT ARGUMENT SHOULD BE REJECTED.

The whole matter pertaining to these examinations at West Point, as well as those at Annapolis, may be summed up in a few sentences :

1st. The conditions of appointment have no relation to the duration or regularity of previous school attendance, application to study, or native capacity.

2d. The table shows that the examinations have been extremely variable, or else that the standard of education throughout the whole country has risen and fallen in curves more fantastic than the fluctuations of the stock market. That which requires a half century to effect appreciably in the general average, has become the variable quantity, and that which can be raised or depressed at will, or accidentally, has become the constant and invariable.

3d. I have shown that these examinations do not indicate even remotely the condition of the common education of the people in different States at the same period, and in consequence that they afford no standard by which we may judge the efficiency of the schools at different periods in the same State.

In our discussion on this point, we have not specially alluded to the graded schools, the so called "all-system schools" of to-day as they are found in the larger towns and cities. To one reading Mr. HINSDALE'S paper from beginning to end, particularly what he has to say on the causes of the "inferiority of our common education," it would seem that the blame for so many failures at West Point falls on them almost exclusively. But the fact is, that, of those who have completed the course of the grammar school with fair success, very few fail at these examinations.

My own testimony may be worth something on this point, and it is to the effect, that although I have had pretty intimate acquaintance with the schools of the two largest cities of this State for twenty years past, I cannot now call to mind even one such failure.

Feeling confident, from my own experience, that if there were any deterioration of our common-school education, it could not be in the graded or "all-system schools," I addressed notes of inquiry to several of the prominent educational men of our own State, that I might ascertain what proportion of failures comes from the thoroughly classified schools of the larger towns and cities. I obtained replies from twenty different parties, representing as many different localities. These parties enumerate sixty-six different individuals whom they know to have made application for admission to the military and naval academies. Out of the sixty-six, only six failed to obtain admission. Of these six, two in one city stood among the lowest thirty out of the hundred eligible candidates in, or from the same school. They were the sons of politicians, low, drinking men, and were appointed for political considerations. In another city, two failed, one a truant who would not go to school if he could help it; the other had been faithful, but lacked mental capacity. In a third city, one failed because he had not completed the grammar-school course. Besides the five above accounted for, there were three others who failed, but they are not included in the sixty-six candidates, for the reason that it is not certainly known whether they came from graded or ungraded schools. Thus it appears that the failures of which Prof. CHURCH and the Board of Visitors complain do not come, as a general thing, from the graded schools, and that the few failures which may be charged against them are the consequences of corrupt or ill considered appointments. It certainly cannot be said that the parties testifying are not competent or reliable witnesses.*

I quote a few of the more pointed remarks made by these gentlemen, with some extended passages especially from the letters of Prof. DeWolf and President E. E. White, of Asbury University, to whom I have referred on a previous page.

Dr. Hancock, formerly Superintendent of the Schools of Cincinnati, now of Dayton, President elect of the National Education Association, speaks thus plainly: "I have no personal knowledge of a single case in which a candidate from the public schools, for either West Point or Annapolis, failed on a regular examination for admission. The standard for admission to West Point has been so much raised within later years, that all Prof. CHURCH says in regard to the preparation of candidates now, as compared with that of candidates fifty years ago, is the merest twaddle."

Superintendent R. W. Stevenson, of Columbus, says: " Not one person receiving his preparation in the public schools of this city has ever failed or been conditioned in any branch of study. This covers a period of thirty years."

* The names of the gentlemen referred to are: Samuel Findley, Pres't A. Schuyler, John H. Brennrman, G. A. Carnahan, Hon. Chas. S. Smart, Gro. W. Stevenson, Dr. John Hancock, H. M. Parker, W. W. Ross, G. W. Walker, President I. W. Andrews, President Jas. H. Fairchild, Prof. D. F. DeWolf, Hon. J. J. Burns, M. R. Andrews, E. F. Moulton, Geo. S. Ormsby and T. J. Wilrs. The names are given in the order in which the cities they represent would stand alphabetically arranged.

President I. W. ANDREWS, of Marietta, has held his present position at the head of one of the oldest and most substantial colleges of the State for more than twenty years. He has been a close observer of educational affairs nearly forty years. His sagacity is beyond question. After enumerating the young men who had received their elementary instruction in the public schools of Marietta, and who have been admitted to West Point and the Naval Academy at Annapolis, President ANDREWS says: "I am glad you are looking into this subject, and would be pleased to know your conclusions. The statement of Prof. CHURCH has been incomprehensible to me."

Prof. D. F. DeWolf, formerly Superintendent of Instruction in Toledo, and now Professor of Modern Languages and Rhetoric in Western Reserve College, concludes his letter as follows : "In short, knowing as I do that for many years, until quite recently the appointments have been made, in our·region, wholly on political grounds, the persons concerned carefully *avoiding* an open market and the selection of the fittest, or the giving of the fittest an opportunity to make known their fitness, I do not regard the examinations or standing of candidates thus taken from the public schools as giving any indication of the kind of work done in these schools. When, as at the time of the last appointment, competitive examinations have been held, the public schools have not suffered in comparison with other schools. Among some eighteen examined then, I *know* of but *one* who was not of the public schools. This one must have been a sophomore in one of our colleges of this State that call other colleges significant names, and yet in this competitive examination an under-graduate of a public school received the appointment, and quite a number of them stood higher than he. Several public schools of the district (Congressional) had representatives among the last number. Yet I do not take that alone as an indication of inferior work in that college. I said above this man must have been a sophomore, because he has since graduated from his college, and I am quite sure the examination occurred three years ago next spring."

8

Hon. E. E. WHITE, now President of Purdue University, speaking of the same subject, says : * * * "I have known several young men appointed to West Point, and most of these were pupils in public schools. It is my impression that all who stood well in the public schools were admitted. Several who attended school irregularly or for other causes failed to maintain a good rank were either not admitted or failed as students after admission, I believe this has been the general experience.

"Permit me to add, that while I do not question Prof. CHURCH's ability as a teacher, or his candor as a man, I doubt the correctness of his statement. He is undoubtedly confident that his judgment is correct, but I do not believe that he has sufficient data to make such a judgment. The standard of admission to West Point is not the same that it was forty years ago, and besides, the method of examining applicants has greatly changed. It was formerly oral ; it is now largely written, if I am correctly informed.   ●

"I have been an examiner of pupils and teachers most of the time for twenty-five years, and I would not undertake to compare the results of an oral examination with those of a written examination. The tests are very different. * * * Again and again have classes, that passed creditably oral tests, failed to pass a written test, intended to be no more severe or difficult.

"In my recent trip to Europe, I crossed the ocean, going and returning, in company with four West Point instructors. I took special pains to learn from them the present method of examining applicants at West Point, and the changes in the tests within their knowledge and experience. The result of these conversations was a conviction that no one can compare the scholarship of present applicants with that of applicants examined twenty years ago, much less forty years ago. What safe comparison, for instance, can be made between the results of a spelling test, consisting of one hundred or more words pronounced successively to a number of applicants, and another test requiring each applicant to write a part of one of Webster's speeches, or an extract from Milton, dictated orally? * * *

"I have used the written method for nearly twenty-five years, and I have preserved many sets of the questions used, and, in a considerable number of cases, the results. It is my impression that young people now going out from our schools, cipher, spell and write better than they did twenty-five years ago. There has certainly been a decided improvement in reading. I am however obliged to add, that the elementary training of the schools is still poor enough to demand better teaching."

Such is the testimony of educators who have had occasion to notice the qualifications of young men who have been sent up to the great national Military and Naval Schools. But on this point we have other testimony from West Point than Prof. CHURCH's.

Prof. MICHIE, in a private letter already referred to, writes that "within a few years past some Congressmen have thrown the position open for competition, and in most cases that have impressed me, I believe the successful competitor is from the common or high school of his district.*

Speaking further on this subject, Prof. MICHIE says:

" I may say that we have had several graduates of the Cincinnati High Schools as cadets, who have all taken very high rank in their classes. The same may be said of the New York Free Academy (now the College of the City of New York) and I doubt not the fact would have been established in the cases of most of our high graduates, that they have had all the advantages of public school education in their youth."

Of the unclassified or common district schools I cannot say much. That there has been some improvement in them within the last fifteen or twenty years cannot be questioned. But the progress of reformation is not uniform in different sections even of the same State, and at best it is everywhere very slow. The standard of education for millions of youth cannot be raised easily, nor in a short time. Majorities for needed school legislation must first be obtained. Every step of advancement has to be lost many a time before it can be finally held. For illustration, though sane men would not attempt any other work of like magnitude without employing the best experts to direct and supervise

---

*The representatives of this congressional district should be especially mentioned as having always opened these appointments to public competition, and the uniform result has been that the prize has been gained by a public school boy, and *no one sent has been rejected.* I believe only one has failed to complete the course.

every agency by which it was carried on, yet the friends of education have been battling for thirty years or more for county
supervision. Mechanics of the lowest grade are required to serve
an apprenticeship before they are permitted to go into a shop,
though they are there subject to constant oversight ; yet, without
so much as a day's special preparation for the important work
which awaits them, teachers are employed annually in thousands of schools that are never visited by a competent inspector.
It is only by the most tedious process that one generation of
teachers after another can be raised up, each only a little better
than the preceding one. Since the beginning of the educational
reformation, which was inaugurated only forty years ago, such a
work could be no more than initiated at comparatively few points.
But while this movement has been so tardy, the standard of
requirement for admission to the Military Academy, even "within
the same scope," may be raised fifty or five hundred per cent. in
a single hour's consultation of the Academic Board. It is undeniable that it has been considerably raised, and the result only
shows that it has been raised more rapidly than the standard of
education throughout the country. This being the case, as we
have shown by incontestable evidence, it is not strange that there
should be a great increase in the number of rejections.

But may it not be that these schools, with all their faults, have
been unfairly judged? May it not be that the examinations now
are as much too severe as they used to be too lax ? Examiners
are not always judicious. See what HERBERT SPENCER says of
various examinations that have found a place in his note-book. I
do not speak here in behalf of the great classified schools ; we
have seen that they take very good care of themselves. We are
now considering the case of Mr. HINSDALE's model schools : the
"no-system" schools of the country districts. But hear what Mr.
SPENCER says of examinations :

      * * * "Our attention is arrested by the general fact that examiners, and
especially those appointed under recent systems of administration, habitually
put questions of which a large proportion are utterly inappropriate. As I learn
from his son, one of our judges not long since found himself unable to answer
an examination-paper that had been laid before law-students. A well known
Greek scholar, editor of a Greek play, who was appointed examiner, found
that the examination-paper set by his predecessor was too difficult for him.

Mr. FROUDE, in his inaugural address to St. Andrews, describing a paper set by an examiner in English History, said, 'I could myself have answered two questions out of a dozen,' and I learn from Mr. G. H. LEWIS that he could not give replies to the questions on English literature which the Civil Service examiners had put to his son, joining which testimonies with kindred ones coming from students and professors on all sides, we find the really noteworthy thing to be that examiners, instead of setting questions fit for students, set questions which make manifest their own extensive learning. Especially if they are young, and have reputations to make or to justify, they seize the occasion for displaying their erudition, regardless of the interests of those they examine." *

How far these remarks may apply to the examinations at West Point we do not know. Possibly they may be wholly inapplicable, but surely one ought to know before he makes any deduction either from the results of one examination or from a series of examinations.

President HINSDALE, turning from the further discussion of the West Point examinations, says: "Perhaps (the evidence submitted) does not prove a deterioration of the common-school education of the country. Perhaps evidence to justify that assertion has not been accumulated, or does not exist." In this we are disposed to agree with him; but let us pass to the latter part of the same paragraph, in which he proposes to comment upon some of the tendencies of the system which he avows to be wrong : "What some of these tendencies are," he says, "will appear as I point out some of the causes of the inferiority of our elementary instruction." Without calling attention to the facility with which he assumes the very thing to be true which he allows may not be proved, and without any comment on his use of "elementary instruction" here, and "common education" on the next page, as synonymous expressions, we have to say that the causes which he points out for the one or the other as he pleases, do not particularly concern us just here. We shall not plead that our boys of to-day do not learn so much as those of two or three generations ago because many of them are children of foreign immigrants ; nor because the time now devoted to school attendance is so much less than it used to be ; nor because "study at home was once the constant rule, and now the infrequent exception ;" nor

---

*Study of Sociology, American Edition, p. 97.

because our children are "absorbed in the distractions of business, of politics and social life;" nor because they "eagerly read
the papers for exciting news." We straightly deny the "inferiority," and have no need of the excuses. On the contrary, we
claim, so far as these grounds of alleged inferiority may be true,
that they be set over to our credit, not as reasons for a miserable
inferiority, but as obstacles to a more glorious success.

But we are more interested to follow President HINSDALE and
Prof. PEABODY as they leave the material and approach the
schools. They complain that the graded school system is exceedingly rigid and inelastic. By this they undoubtedly mean that
pupils can be advanced from class to class only at regular intervals of time and that the bright pupil, the mediocre and the dullard are advanced alike. President HINSDALE says :

"Its tendency is to stretch all the pupils on the same bedstead." * * *
"Then the tendency of the graded schools is to sacrifice the brightest children
to the dullards or to the mediocres. The dullest cannot be made to keep pace
with the brightest, where the latter are going at their normal pace ; but the
best can be made to go as slowly as the dullest, or, if the ability of the dullard
be not the standard of achievement, then it is the ability of the mediocre. In
no case do or can the brightest minds have a fair chance."

This point is certainly worthy of most careful consideration not
only in this discussion, but always, especially in the practical
management of schools, whether graded or ungraded. Every
child has a right to the normal development of his mind according to his native capacity. To stunt the mind is no less criminal
than to stunt the body. If the graded school be obnoxious
to this charge, it matters not what it may offer in compensation,
let us go back to the "no-system" schools of former periods or the
rural district schools of to-day and if they do not give opportunity
for the growth of "a man" let them too "be smashed," let us
throw away all our grand schemes of education, and begin again.

But does the objection hold ?   Let us look into the schools and
take an extreme case.   A class of fifty boys is before us ; they are
all studying arithmetic, grammar, geography; they all read and
spell.   Let us examine into their case, and ascertain how many of
them appear to be retarded by their association with stupid companions.   Here we have some records at hand which show exactly

what we shall find. Some of them stand from fifty to sixty in arithmetic and seventy to eighty in grammar. Others stand eighty-five to ninety in the former and sixty to seventy in the latter. Now who suffers by the association of the class ? Not the most brilliant. The one who stands highest has perhaps ninety. Now ninety means that he has failed entirely on one question out of ten, or parts of two or more questions. That is, he has exerted his utmost power, "blood and training" have done their best and yet there is more to do. But how about the dullard ? He stands perhaps forty or fifty on a scale of one hundred. Have his interests been sacrificed for his brighter companions ? The probability is that even he has spent so much time in the study, review and re-review of the matter gone over that he has absorbed all the information and acquired all the discipline of which his sluggish nature is capable.

Sixty, seventy-five and ninety stand for all the acquisitions of three different boys, which can be represented by percentages. Is that all ? Far from it. One has learned only that which lies upon the surface of things. A few facts of science have a lodgment in his memory more or less permanent, according to the power of his retentive faculty. His knowledge is superficial and cannot be otherwise, because his reasoning power is feeble. The mediocre understands your rules and applies them and by dint of study he masters some of their principles. In the meantime the brighter boys possess themselves of process and principle and gain an insight into the deeper relation of things. You have done for the three boys what was most profitable for each. By the very classification which has been objected to, you have stimulated the sluggish boy up to his highest capacity, and you have compelled and habituated the bright boy to dwell upon a subject of study till it is understood according to the strength and maturity of his intellect. But there is yet something more than the mastering even of broadest principles, in which all are exercised alike, but with very different results. There is a clearness of statement, readiness, precision and power in the use of language which goes for much in the intercourse of the world, and certainly quite as much in the development of mind.

I have spoken of the boys who are regularly advanced from year to year with their class, but with vastly different degrees of excellence and as widely different results as to general culture. But there are two extremes of which I have not spoken. There is the dullard who fails to be advanced with his class. He falls back into the class which was below him. The advocate of the "no-system" school cries out that "it is unjust to keep him back six months for a deficiency which he might make up in one." If the page of a text book or the line of a syllabus were the standard by which his mastery of a subject is to be determined we should ·grant its injustice. It would be stretching *some*, though not all, "on the same bedstead." But there is a maximum and a minimum to be gained within the same scope of study and no one will deny that the maximum of attainment which may be reached in any one class is at least of equal value to the merely passable minimum of the next higher. Then there are some of superior mental endowments but backward in their studies who come into your graded schools at an advanced age. From what President HINSDALE says, it might be supposed that they would be allowed to move forward only at the slow pace of their younger associates. The supposition, however, would be possible only to those who know nothing of the practical workings of the graded schools under ordinarily judicious management. The truth is that pupils are promoted in graded schools, as well as others, whenever it becomes apparent that they can be advanced without prejudice to health or sound scholarship. In the city of Cleveland—I speak of it only by way of illustration—hundreds are thus put forward every year. Of about three hundred and fifty admitted to the High Schools last summer, nearly fifty went in, in advance of the classes with which they had been associated only a year or two before. Of the graduates of the High Schools at last annual commencement, one, a boy, entered the D grammar. class only two and a half years previous; another, a girl, only about live or six years ago entered the B Primary.* These however are extreme cases of rapid advancement, as there are on the other hand extreme

*It may seem a little remarkable in view of what Prof. PRABODY says of the superior 'capacity of children "having generations of culture behind them," that the parents of neither of these pupils lay any special claims to culture.

cases of tardy progress. Between these extremes there is play enough to show that the complaints that the graded school system is "rigid," "inelastic," "tyrannous," "a procrustean bed," etc., etc., are not founded on prevailing facts.

Closely connected with its alleged inelasticity, just noticed, is the objection that the graded-school system requires a uniformity of training and discipline, "which tends for the time being, as much as possible, to wipe out all individual differences, to destroy individual ambition, and to produce in the end, as Mr. ELIOT says, an average product, a sort of mental, moral and physical mean standard, which has been obtained quite as much by stunting what is good in the children educated, as by forcing work out of the dull." *

Inasmuch as this is a merely speculative view of the probable result of our graded-school systems, I shall give it but little attention.

It is only another form of an old argument which was once urged against the Military and Naval Academies : an argument which has been utterly discredited by the history of those two great arms of national defence. Precisely the same argument was originally used against Normal schools. It was said of the latter that they would tend to repress individuality, and train up teachers of only respectable mediocrity. This too has been disproved by experience. An argument something like this used to be urged against allowing pupils to write after engraved copies, because it would destroy that individuality of hand-writing, which it was said "was the only safeguard against forgery," etc. Had these argument proved to be of any worth, it might seem advisable to meet the objections now urged against graded schools. As it is, we may safely pass to another point. In the meantime, let us take heart from the lesson which nature teaches. The oak tree and the blackberry bush are called to life by the same sun; they have been nourished by the same earth for thousands of years; yet both blackberry bush and oak tree have maintained their individualities to this day.

*The Nation No. 517, as quoted by President HINSDALE.

9

The classification of a school, be it large or small, is arranging in a class or grade all the pupils who can receive instruction together with advantage. If this classification be made carefully, and with a full knowledge of the ability of the pupils as well as their advancement in their studies, it is likely to be permanent for the majority of them. For none however is it a cast-iron arrangement which cannot be altered. As we have seen, some pupils soon demonstrate their ability to go forward to the next higher class, and others show that they are too weak to keep pace with their associates. In the class above or below, these find their level and the work for which they are fitted by natural capacity and habits of study.

The original purpose of the arrangement was to enable teachers to gain time for attention to the work of each class and of each individual member of a class. How much more readily and thoroughly this may be done than in the ungraded school, can easily be understood even by one who is not habituated to look into such matters. By way of illustration: let there be fifty pupils all in one class; call it a "platoon," or any other obnoxious name you please. All are studying the same problems in percentage; all read, spell and recite geography and grammar together. The teacher, having only four or five subjects of instruction, studies her lessons more exhaustively than her pupils. She knows just where every difficulty lies, and how it is to be met. Let us suppose that an arithmetic lesson is to be heard or given. A certain part of the work, some principle or other, perhaps, needs to be explained. By a few rapid questions the teacher finds out what all know, what some do and others do not, and what none know. The work that needs to be done for all is done, it may be, in five or ten minutes, while in an ungraded school, where each pupil is in a class by himself, it would take a whole forenoon to do the same amount of work for each, and it would have to be done under the disadvantage of many being idle while waiting for needed help, or under the pretence of needing it. The explanation for all being thus given in a few minutes, and for sections of the class according to their needs in a few more, the inspection of the work of all, and individual instruction where it is required, begins ; and in an hour all is done, and well done, that otherwise would have been very poorly done in a day. For every subject taught, the advantage is the same not only to the whole "platoon," but to each individual. The truth is, that for forty or fifty pupils, the only place where anything like individual instruction can be had is in the thoroughly graded school.

What is said, on this point, in that most excellent pedagogical library, the "Encyclopedia of Education," applies to the whole question at issue.

"Heterogeneous masses of children cannot be instructed simultaneously. They may be made to perform mechanically certain school exercises; may perhaps be taught to read, to spell, to write and to cipher to some extent; but it can only be by rote, without the due exercise of their intelligence, and hence without proper mental development. A poorly classified school can never be really efficient, whatever talent in teaching may be brought to bear upon it."

Classification has another advantage, which is conceded it by Mr. HINSDALE. I refer to division of labor. The highest skill in any one branch of instruction, and I am almost disposed to add at any stage thereof, can be reached only in a thoroughly classified school.

The graded school is not the thought of to-day, nor of those who are now engaged in the work of teaching. In all its features, it was advocated years ago by men who in their youth had experienced all the disadvantages of the ungraded schools of two or three generations past. They knew by sad experience that the kind of individual instruction—individual neglect rather—which they themselves had received, could not lift the schools out of the depths into which they had fallen. They saw clearly that even Normal schools would be of little avail, unless the common schools could be so organized that time might be gained for something more than hurried *memoriter* repetitions of rules and definitions, and the almost unguided, solitary work of the scholar.

If proof is wanting of the superior efficiency of classified schools, it may be found in the fact that wherever they have sprung up, however defective they may have been at the start, private schools have failed at once; or, if they have survived for a time, unless

in hands of teachers of exceptional ability, they have soon become subjects for ridicule. The private school, and even the
endowed academy throughout the whole country, is going down
before the graded-school system. Every town of one thousand
inhabitants and upwards used to support many of them. Now
they can have a healthy existence only in the largest cities.

But Mr. HINSDALE says "there is a wide-spread dissatisfaction
with the results of the prevalent system." We have shown elsewhere how various and contradictory the causes of dissatisfaction
are. That they should be so is not wonderful, for the common
schools touch more nearly the deepest interests of the human
heart than any other secular institution. The principles of education are not generally understood. The father and the mother see
that their children are not taught as they were ; and if incapacity
or other causes prevent progress, the blame is very naturally laid
to the changes in the methods of instruction. Hence dissatisfaction does not exist to any great degree among the parents
of the bright children. But whether it exist among one class or
another, it is well that it does exist somewhere, for there is nothing more certain than this, that dissatisfaction is an incen-
tive to improvement. If, however, men avail themselves of this
dissatisfaction to incite discontent and produce reaction, though
they may succeed for a time as reactionists have done, they will
find that what was dissatisfaction will in the end become devotion.

But Mr. HINSDALE suggestively raises the question whether the
public school is "the best place for a man to put his bright boy
or girl, if he happens to have a bright one." In answer to this
question, I can only say that it is no uncommon thing for
men of intelligence to seek out the private school for the weak-
ling of the flock, while the brighter and more ambitious children
are sent to the public school. An eminent physician of this city
but recently told me that he has noticed this as a very common
practice in the families which he visits. The common opinion on
this point is well illustrated by an incident recently related to
me, of an earnest, studious daughter of wealthy parents in our
city, who, when it was proposed to send her to a private school

with a sister who was notably deficient in intellect, said: "Oh, that school will do well enough for (we will say) Mattie, but I hope you don't think it's the place for me."

But notwithstanding we appreciate so highly the superiority of the graded schools as compared with the unclassified, we do not think that they are without defect nor do we think that they are "ideal" places for the education either of bright boy or dullard,* for who is there on earth that has practically realized an institution so fair that the mind of man may not conceive a fairer?

No, the public school is not claimed to be perfect. High above all existing, all possible systems, there is "a model which we may approach in a greater or less degree but which is yet infinitely distant," and as our progress is upward this ideal will forever recede until it merges into the absolute and perfect. Men may forever struggle to reach it, but it will forever be infinitely distant.

But we are not content to disclaim any notion that our graded schools are perfect. We go further and say that they are not as good as they can be made; that, as Prof. HINSDALE says, "they need much criticism and revision." Let us enumerate only a few of their principal faults.

1. They are not adapted as they might be to the preparation of the young for the different avocations of life. For example: the young man who has an ambition to take respectable rank among the mechanics of the future should, before he leaves the High School, be well advanced in the mathematics and other sciences on which his success must mainly depend. Even in the Grammar school grades, some differences should be made between the course of study of those who are going into mercantile or mechanical pursuits and those who are destined for a literary or professional career. The former especially need the sciences, the latter the classics.

2. The classes in our graded schools are generally too large; and, singular as it may seem, those that have the highest reputation are the most liable to objection on this score. Their managers pay high salaries that they may obtain the most efficient

_____

*KANT said, "What I have termed an *ideal* was in Plato's philosophy an idea of the Divine mind." Meiklejohn's Translation, *Critique of Pure Reason.*

teachers, and then, to compensate, give them too many pupils to teach. If you must have large classes to justify the employment of the best teachers, there can be no doubt of this being the better policy. But the wisdom of the future will require that while we sacrifice nothing in the quality of the teacher we must gain by reducing the number of children under her care by at least one-half. But this will be possible only when education is estimated at something like its true worth.

3. The course of study in these schools is not adapted to the best education of the pupils. This is especially true of the grammar grades in which an attempt is made to teach too much of arithmetic and grammar. Time is wasted in fruitless efforts to teach what can not be comprehended by the youth of ten to fourteen years of age while that which he could understand and which would be of greater use in ˌhis daily business and social life is neglected.

4. In country towns and village districts having a few hundred children, and sometimes in places of larger pretensions, uneducated and superficial men are sometimes put upon boards of education; incompetent or inexperienced teachers are employed to be changed year by year; a full course of study ranging from primary to high school is developed, generally in imitation of some large city, and the effigy of a graded system is then hung up for the ridicule of our critics while the more judicious mourn. This is a free country, the forms of law have been complied with and who shall say nay? It is the graded school thus organized and administered that brings discredit upon the whole public-school system, just as our co-called colleges and universities bring discredit upon the cause of higher education. It is such institutions as these that send up boys to the Military and Naval Academies who profess to have studied sciences, the names of which they cannot spell. Truly the public schools do need much criticism and revision, if these be the specimens by which you judge of their defects; but you might as properly judge the artists of England by the execution of the sign-boards which swing in front of her public houses.

5. But the faults in the well-graded public schools, which cannot be corrected for want of a public sentiment to sustain the

somewhat radical changes which would be necessary to effect
reform, and the graver faults of those half-classified schools, which
make pretences of impossible courses of study at the expense of
thoroughness at every point—these faults are not the only ones
which we feel bound to acknowledge. There are very common
faults, which might be corrected in a good degree if intelligent
and determined men were always put upon Boards of Education,
and if such men were duly sustained by the people in the perform-
ance of their duties. Such are the faults which result from the
employment of incompetent teachers, faults of organization and
administration, faults of plans of study. Finally, making one
broad admission, we confess that the graded schools are scored
all over with the faults which are incident to all human affairs.

THE FORMALISM OF THE SCHOOLS.

President HINSDALE, in speaking of the schools of New England a century or half a century ago, quotes from Dr. PEABODY
as follows:

" There was no arbitrary or fixed arrangement of classes or plan of classification, but each scholar was virtually a class by himself, in some studies
perhaps reciting alone, often out of school hours, in others associated with
different companions, according to his or her proficiency."

Mr. HINSDALE then continues:

"Now all this is changed. In place of an inartificial method or no method,
we have an educational liturgy—each gospel, collect, psalm and prayer attended
by its appropriate rubric." Against the current formalism of teachers he di-
rects some of his hardest blows. He says he has " heard every member of a
class of twenty obliged to repeat separately ' one bean and two beans are three
beans.' Also, that he had listened to an object lesson in which the teacher
' spent several minutes in demonstrating, with a wonderful affluence of illustration, to children six or seven years old, that the horse had four legs and a
child but two.'"

To this, I would only make such reply as would occur to the
ordinary reader, that because Dr. PEABODY had happened to see
these things it don't go very far to prove that they are common or
essential to a graded-school system. For one, I have never seen
anything approach the silliness of the "demonstration" spoken
of. As to the repetition of " one bean and two beans are three

beans," it may have seemed necessary to a very sensible and excellent teacher to require such a thing in some particular case, yet I think *I have never heard any one do it.*

But let us do justice. Is it not altogether likely that Prof. PEABODY introduced these incidents for the purpose of enlivening an afternoon's discourse before a teachers' association rather than to demonstrate any inherent defect of the prevalent public school system? Has not President HINSDALE mistaken his design? One would suppose it possible, from the very singular misapprehension which he exhibits in the very next sentence:

"A friend of mine" he says, "was once looking through the schools of a city very proud of her schools. In pointing out some noteworthy features of one of them, the supervising principal called attention to the fact that it required but three minutes after the bell struck to empty the building of its hundreds of occupants. *As though the time consumed by a child in walking down stairs were an important feature of a school!*"*

We should hardly know whether Mr. HINSDALE is serious just here, if it were not for the gravity of the next sentence, viz:

"Here we are dealing with every day criticisms on the common schools, and it is proper to inquire how far they are just, and how far the features complained of can be removed."

Shall I be wanting in respect to our very worthy and highly-esteemed associate, if I should say that he had written a passage here which eclipses the silliness of the exercises to which Dr. PEABODY refers in the paragraph previously quoted? Is it necessary to explain that time saved in the movement of large bodies of pupils is time saved to each one for study and instruction; that the rapid and orderly assembling and dismissing of a thousand or fifteen hundred pupils every day of a school year, six times per day, without accident to the feeble and the timid, is a matter of no little importance? Finally, is it necessary that we should demonstrate the necessity of such training in case of panic produced by alarm of fire, † etc.? Were I to attempt it, the intelligent

---

*The italics are ours.

† It was only a few days after the delivery of President HINSDALE'S address that we heard through the newspapers of an incident which shows the value of just such discipline. A large school house at Minneapolis is said to have caught fire in such a way as almost to cut off retreat. By the presence of mind of the teachers and the daily habit of the pupils all were saved without injury.

reader might look upon me as trying to rival the teacher before spoken of, who "spent several minutes in demonstrating * * * to children six or seven years old, that a horse had four legs and a child but two." But seriously, may it not be that this rigid economy of time, now exercised in our best public schools, enables them to do much more work than was done in the schools of the past, when teachers, as Mr. HINSDALE implies, took less pride in saving the minutes.

Again, on the second page from that on which we find the passages above quoted, Mr. HINSDALE returns to the same subject. Here he speaks as follows: "Then there is the teacher's tendency to formalism and routine. Several years ago, I discovered that an elaborate school ritual had been evolved, and I am gratified that Dr, PEABODY speaks of a school 'ritual and rubric.' He says he has seen a 'fourth part of the time given to a reading or spelling lesson occupied in meaningless evolutions and gestures performed by the scholars in the interval between leaving their seats and their resting in their final positions in front of the desk,' as who has not ?"

We suppose that Mr. HINSDALE will allow that a somewhat specific course of study, written or unwritten, is indispensable if we are to have graded schools at all. We believe he says as much, but he appears to think it a sort of necessary evil. He seems to hold that the unclassified school of a century or half a century ago had the advantage in that its teachers were not trammeled by any fixed course or syllabus of instruction.

In the consideration of this as well as other questions, we must keep pertinent facts clearly in mind. In the first place, there is not now, and there never has been, more than one teacher in a thousand who is qualified to plan and manage the work from the beginning to the end of an elementary education. To do this well, one must have reached the period of maturity; he must have been a careful observer of the processes of mental growth ; he must have a keen insight into child life ; he must be thoroughly conversant with the subjects of study. In order that he may go in the right direction, the planner should see the end from the beginning, and thereafter each step must be taken with due regard

10

to what has gone before, and what is to follow. There are very few teachers who can fulfill these conditions; but though all were competent there must be unity of design from first to last.

A harmonious development of all the faculties of a child, and a right selection and sequence of studies to be pursued from infancy almost to manhood, forbid that there should be frequent or radical changes in the general plan. But with frequent changes of teachers this is inevitable, unless there be a general plan for all to follow. The views of different individuals conflict as to the true order of studies, and it is even a question among men as to what education is. To illustrate: one holds that to teach reading, writing and ciphering is the sole end for which elementary schools were established; another party maintains that the three "R's," as indispensable as they may be, do not, as generally taught, tend to lift the mind or heart to a higher plane of action. One holds that the chief purpose of studying grammar is to learn its technicalities, and gain discipline of intellect by means of parsing and analysis; another holds all this in light esteem compared with carefully-directed practice in the use of language. It is commonly thought that arithmetic should precede geometry; but there are some who would reverse the process. Now, it won't do to hand over a child, much less a whole school, at intervals of not more than three or five years, to successive teachers holding such opposite views, "to plan and manage their own work." We find frequent changes of teachers inevitable, whether they be men or women, for in these degenerate days the call of better pay is as effectual as the call of the marriage bell. How then shall unity of design in the fabric of education be guaranteed? We reply, in only one way, and that is by laying out our plans and specifications before the structure is commenced. The old analogy herein implied is defective in many particulars, but it will suffice for our present purpose. A well-defined course of study, then, would seem to be a vital necessity to the unclassified as well as the graded school.

But is a school having a course of study, or a syllabus of instruction, or a time table which indicates the relative importance of the several branches pursued, more justly chargeable with formalism than the old-time school, such as we have had before us

in the testimony which has been submitted ? The difference between the two may be briefly stated as follows : The teacher who
is guided only by a course, a syllabus, a time table, is left to his
own judgment as to *how* he shall teach the successive topics
required. But, when the programme of work is lacking, the book
regulates the course of study. It prescribes not alone the order of
topics but the exact form in which definition, demonstration and
rule are to be learned ; and if it be not in the hands of a true
master of the art of teaching, he who should be the master becomes the most abject of slaves. The Board of Education, then,
that lays down a course of study leaves its teachers pretty much
at liberty in their method of teaching. The Board that simply
prescribes a book, orders the method by which it shall be taught ;
that is, the method of the book. To which may formalism be
charged, with the greater justice?

We have often heard teachers, by way of apology for failure,
say that they could not teach unless they were allowed to teach
in their own way, but we never heard such a declaration from the
mouth of one who could teach anything without the book in hand :
that is, do anything more than *hear recitations.*

MULTIPLICITY OF STUDIES AND SUPERFICIALITY.

There is a very common impression that more studies are now
pursued in the public schools than at any previous time, but the
truth is that the maximum was reached twenty or twenty-five
years ago. For instance : besides all the branches now taught,
algebra and physiology were studied in the higher classes of the
schools of Cleveland and Cincinnati from 1850 to 1855, and perhaps later. The tendency since that time has been to reduce
rather than to extend the course. Then there is a very common
misapprehension also as to the extent to which the so-called
higher branches are taught in some of the lower grades. For
example : when people who are not familiar with the schools come
to hear that physics is taught to children of twelve and thirteen
years of age, they picture to themselves these young children
studying and making regular recitations on these subjects from
the ordinary treatises, such as were studied by themselves when

they were at the academy or college. But this is not the true
picture. It should rather be, of the teacher giving a half-hour's
lesson or holding a familiar conversation, once or twice per week,
on a line of subjects which properly fall under the head of
physics. The instruction given is not scientific, it dwells only
upon those phenomena which may very appropriately engage the
attention of mere children. For instance : by a few simple experi-
ments which require no more apparatus than can be found in
every school room, such as the drinking cup, the water pail, etc.,
these boys and girls can be made to understand that air occupies
space, has weight, and rises, when warmed to a temperature higher
than the surrounding atmosphere. The ventilation of a room
can be explained and even the cause of winds can be made plain.
The reason why we speak of higher and lower temperatures
can be shown by exposing the thermometer alternately to cold
and heat. The expansion of metals under high temperature can
be easily demonstrated, and why the thermometer rises and falls
as the temperature changes.

So I might go on enumerating phenomena under the head of
those great names, mechanics, hydraulics, etc., etc., in all of
which the child may be interested, and every one of which will
stimulate his observing faculties, excite thought and add to his
intelligence. No cramming of lessons to be recited again, needs
or ought to be attempted. The only aim is to make the child
an intelligent boy or girl. What he learns will aid him in all his
other studies, and if he leave school at an early age, will be of
service to him when he goes into the workshop and in his intercourse with men. He may or may not be given to understand
that he is learning " physics," but he really is, and that to good
purpose, if he is rightly taught.

In drawing this paper to a close, I have not the space to
discuss the question whether this is superficial in an obnoxious
sense. I would here merely raise the inquiry whether such teach-
ng is more superficial than learning that the atmosphere is very
cold about the tops of high mountains ; that there are trade winds,
political boundary lines, tropic circles, and a thousand other
things, without learning their causes. The age has come for
these children to see and know what there is about them affecting

their daily life, though they cannot comprehend the philosophy of things.

The age of abstract reason has not come to these children yet, and any attempt to call the faculty into any more than feeble exercise must prove futile—worse indeed than useless. It is therefore amusing to hear Prof. CHURCH speak of training "the minds of *beginners* in the *logical reasoning* required in arithmetic and grammar." But though a very superficial remark, it suggests that some grave mistakes are made in our common schools. They are not however the mistakes which he imagines.

What some of these mistakes may be, will appear as we compare the present course of study with that which prevailed three-quarters of a century ago. Spelling, reading, writing, arithmetic, and English grammar, including epistolary correspondence, were then required.' The same subjects are taught to-day, with the addition of geography, music, drawing, and, for the higher classes, History of the United States. Besides these, instruction in natural science, such as we have just spoken of, is commenced. That these additions do not preclude increased attention to the original list, becomes apparent on taking note of the amount of work done in the olden time as compared with what is now accomplished in what are called the common school studies. We have already seen that though the object of our present study of spelling is widely different from what it used to be, the time given it by each pupil is about the same. Passing this, we next come to reading. The Bible (mostly the Psalms and the New Testament) and "Webster's Third Part" were the books then used. Comparing these with the readers now in use, we cannot doubt that our pupils are now expected to read in course twice or three times as much matter as was then required, to say nothing of the reading which has to be done in the added studies, geography and history.

In arithmetic, it is quite certain, that more than twice as many rules and from three to five times more problems are required now than formerly. SALEM TOWN tells us that fractions were out of the question about the beginning of the present century, and his testimony on this point is confirmed by many other witnesses. In the tenth edition of Adams' arithmetic, which was

ERRATA.

On page 64, second paragraph,—President E. E. WHITE of "Asbury" University, should read President E. E. WHITE of "Purdue" University.

On same page, in the foot-note, the name of the Superintendent of Instruction, Columbus, Ohio, should be "R. W. STEVENSON," not "GEO. W. STEVENSON," and the name of the Superintendent of the Schools of Zanesville, should be "A. T. WILES," not "T. J. WILES."

On page 79, fourth line from bottom, the proof reader has "don't" for "does not."

www.ingramcontent.com/pod-product-compliance
Lightning Source LLC
Chambersburg PA
CBHW031450270326
41930CB00007B/937